WORLD-CLASS TRAINING

BREN WHITE

Odenwald Press
Dallas

World-Class Training

Copyright © 1992 by Bren White

Published by Odenwald Press, Dallas, Texas

Library of Congress Cataloging in Publication Data

White, Bren D., 1957-
    World-class training / Bren D. White.
           p. cm.
    Includes bibliographical references and index.
    ISBN 0-9623216-2-1 : $19.95
    1. Employees—Training of. 2. Competition.
International. I. Title.
    HF5549.5.T7W475   1992
    658.3'124—dc20   92-15225
                                 CIP

Printed in the United States of America

To Cheryl, Stresa, Trieste and Bjorn,
my favorite people in the whole world

Acknowledgements

There are many people around the world who helped me in this four-year project. I can only list some of them here, but I want to thank everyone who was in some way involved in this cutting-edge project. Among those I wish to thank:

My wife Cheryl and our three wonderful children; they were truly a blessing in my struggle to complete this book in my spare time; my parents, Joe and Wanita White, for their global orientation and sense of adventure; Chuck and Delores Nolan; Dr. Jim Windle, my mentor; Quentin Englerth; Dieter Kulicke of Interlake Corporation; Jim Kouzes, president of Tom Peters Group/LS; Lewis Griggs, co-author of *Going International*; Dr. Clyde Austin, Abilene Christian University; Dr. Leonard Nadler, professor emeritus of George Washington University; Dr. Dan Garner, vice president of ICI/Cellmark; Jerry Ralls, director of human resources for Ohmeda/BOC; Dr. Leonard Hill, director of executive development and human resource planning for AMP, Inc.; Art Rodgers, Joe Giusti, Gary Sheetz, David Baker, Don Parrish and Ray Faidley of AMP, Inc.; Bobby Boone, vice president of AT&T, Europe; Nancy Burgas, director of executive development for AT&T; Clyde Prestowitz; Dr. Nancy Adler of McGill University; Jim Gannon, vice president of Royal Bank of Canada; Jim Burge, corporate vice president of Motorola; Bill Wiggenhorn, vice president of Motorola; Ken Patterson of Motorola University; Frank Popoff, CEO of Dow Chemical; Bob Postlethwait, vice president of International for Lilly & Co.; Stephen Rhinesmith; George Renwick; Stephen Day, president of International Venture Associates; Bruce Crockett, CEO of COMSAT; Jack Hannon, vice president of COMSAT; Ron Mario, division president of COMSAT; Dr. John Evans, vice president of COMSAT Labs; Mary Kemp of Maxwell Communications; Lincoln Yarbrough of GE; Wendy Webster of The White House; Lou Kemp; Jane Lanier; Mary Burns; John Vargo, vice president of International for COMSAT; Bill Locke, group vice president of International for Armstrong World; Brian Glade, human resource advisor of International, Texaco; Jeff Kaplan; Joe Fabiano, director of employee relations for Disney; John Christianson of Honda; Lee Ashton of Subaru-Isuzu; Frank Sterrett of British Aerospace; Leslie Pearson of Federal Express; Larry Raskin, manager of training and development for Analog Devices; Linda Heath, director of training for Johnson & Johnson; Matty Petty-Hunter, sales training director for MCI; Bernie Marsh; Peter Burton, founder of CASE Group plc; Jack Reis; Michael Bonsignore, chief operating officer for Honeywell; Mike Hickey of Grand Met; John Flato of Allied Bendix; Gayle Crowe; Kevin Hogg; Dave Keeney; Dr. Phil Gordon of John Hopkins School of Advanced International Studies; Eric Novotny; Jackie Jones, director of training for Millipore; David Luther of Corning; Peter Danos, retired 3M international executive; the employees of Pontiac Motors, Deshler Products, Dutch Boy, CASE Communications, General Physics, COMSAT, and WORLD Group Associates, worldwide;

Warren Bull; Dr. Michael Marquardt; Serge Ogranovitch; Ken Rebeck of RWD; Lori Gillespie; Kermit Hollingsworth; Frank Smith, senior vice president of Black & Decker; Mike Convey, president of Price & Pfister; George Duke, vice president of Alex Brown; Jon Huntsman of Huntsman Chemicals; Jonathan Halperin of FYI; Craig Storti, author of *Art of Crossing Cultures*; Doug Fulmer; Kevin Cornacchio of U.S. Council for International Business; Paul Wineman; Allen Pratt; Shellyn McCaffrey, deputy secretary of international affairs for the U. S. Department of Labor; Steve DeMorro and Diane Yarosz of Squibb; Lee Cole; David Daniel; Gary Selby; Barbara and Bing Lam; Lerrill and Debby White; Dan and Nancy Long; Caskie Lewis; Pam Farr, vice president of human resource planning for Marriott; Dr. John Onto, Associate Dean of Business for Georgetown University; Jerrund Wilkerson of Merck; Jim Ice of Alcoa; Jim Kearney of Sherwin-Williams; Ed Higgenbottom; Tom Brindisi; Mark Cummings, vice president of CASE/Datatel; Dr. Mark Chartrand; Lexie Knowlton Pfetzing of Chubb; Debra Morehouse of Johns Hopkins University; Carol Lyles and Pam Frankhouser of Johns Hopkins University; Carol Keyser of Howard Community College; Sylvia Odenwald; Mary Jo Beebe; Lynn Holt; Mike Duff of TTC; Bill Boden, vice president of human resources for the Rouse Corporation; Dr. Don Gentry, dean of the School of Technology; Phillip McGrath and Carol Morgan of Purdue University; Jack Rutter of Ideas, Inc.; Svend Erik Sorenson; Michael Mkoko; Abdillahi Handulle Mohomud; Gerry Poggi of the University of Maryland; David Paradise; Jack Fox; Byron Lane, associate professor at Pepperdine University; Hia Lin Choo; Gregg Smith of

Audi/Volkswagen; Lance Brady; Lynn Tyler of Brigham Young; Jimmie Smith; Elwy M. El-Gazzar; Beverly Battaglia; Fernando Rovelo Camilo; Patricia Keegan; Dan Williams of British Telecom; Mike Nolan; Margo Cooper and Jodi McGill; Ray Curley; Pierre Casse; Dick Dolliver of General Physics; Lou Guadagnoli; Michael Skarzynski, CEO of American Mercantile Group; Larry Miller; Dale Phillips; Mark Reeves; Evart Cable; Diana Risen of The World Bank; Gregg and Ronna Albritton; Russ and Janeil Neilan; Neal Chalofsky of George Washington University; Joe and Darla Letourneau; Michael Illich; Ernesto Poza; Linda Buggy of Chemical Bank; Jan Jones of Baxter; Gary Heath of Honda; Glenn Youngstedt of Whirlpool; Eva Doyle; Steve Parker of Maxima; Dick Gienopie; Stanley Shipp; Dr. Howard V. Perlmutter of Wharton; Don Dougherty; Glover Shipp; Epi Bilak; Dr. Robert Moran; Gordon Bennett of ABB; Charlie and Edie Seashore; Ray Stata, chairman of Analog Devices; Dean Daniels; Manuel Guitian of IMF; George Hayes; Jeff Luther; Ray Nelson of Procter & Gamble; Dr. Wil Goodheer, president of International Christian University; Bob Grigg; Robert Wussler, former corporate vice president, Turner Broadcasting; Irv Goldstein, chairman of Intelsat; Donna Carew; Robert Baumann; Carl Washenko; Jim Helms; Esmerelda Kirkpatrick; Roy Collins; Wanda McKinley; Ralph Fulchino; Curtis Scott; Cindy Allen; Zena Galloway; Merilee Worsey; Alice Tierney; Patricia Benton; Chris Leber; John Kopinski; Jim Farmer; Bob Hunter; Dick McGraw; Katy Holman; Griff Lee; Janine Anderson-Bays; Chris Arant; Kathleen Abernathy; Betty Alewine; Jay Arnold; Angela Beverly; Alice Bullie; George Bolling; Ted Boll; Laura Bryan;

Dr. Joe Campanella; David Cade; Chris Coady; Linda Bower; Dattakumar Chitre; Cal Cotner; Ruth Gorman; Colin Bathgate; Rhonda Wilcom; Alok Gupta; Bob Gray; Will Cook; Bill Fallon; David Farmer; Steve Skjei; Dorothy Clingman; Bob Yamakazi; Jim Sutton; Chuck Gomez; Joel Alper; Don Flora; Dilip Gokhale; Jim Kasik; Al Yenyo; Kevin Spade; Paul Pizzani; Rose Javier; Evette Fulton; Jim Janeso; Brent Jacocks; Dr. Ivor Knight; Gloria Ford; Nancy Roblin; Jack Oslund; Jerry Breslow; Bill Schnicke; Ranjit Singh; Paul Stern; Bill Everts; Barbara Swaylik; Dan Thomas; Linda Wellstein; Carl Sederquist; Dr. Peter Almquist; Cathy Waters; Gloria Ward; Bernie Joyner; Janice Wilson; Warren Zeger; Allen Flower; Cynthia Cole; Francois Assal; Sandy Clatworthy; Betsy Christie; Diana Johnson; Chris Mason; Amy McIver; Maury Mechanick; David Meadows; Bob Myer; Paul Palmiter; Krishna Pande; Paul Rhee; Diane Rowley; Phyllis Rhoe; Mary Sims; Paul Schrantz; Bill Schmidt; Howard Witt; George Zachman; Frank Famariss; Mary Blasinsky; Russell Fang; Keith Fagan; Art Gelven; Regina Johnson; Scott Giarman; Joe Flynn; Fred Gould; Mary Duvall; Dr. Ben Pontano; Bob Smith; John Upshur; Alfred Goldman; Leslie Downey; Debra Delbianco; Kishor Saralkar; Ed Weisbrot; Patricia Richards; and Pierre, the gateman in Brussels.

Foreword

During the 1980s a new organizational configuration has evolved — the "global company." This company does not operate within national boundaries but instead does business anywhere on the globe where there is a potential market. Global competitiveness has become the challenge of the 1990s.

Perhaps the most powerful means of meeting the competitiveness challenge is "World-Class Training" as masterfully conceived and implemented by Bren White. His approach is a comprehensive and integrated way of continually preparing and regauging the entire organization for long-term competitiveness and global visibility. It artfully weaves all strategically useful training into the larger organizational culture. For example, PC skills, time management, foreign languages, and international negotiating arc designed to serve the strategic purposes of the organization.

World-Class Training reflects the quality of delivery, the global focus of content, and the design used to administer or operate the entire organizational learning process. Bren emphasizes that it is most critical that all training offered in this new strategic process be value-producing and high-quality.

The end result, Bren points out, needs to be both positive and visible to all employees as well as to all customers and competitors. World-Class Training can be the determining factor in global competitiveness. World-class manufacturing, world-class customer service, world-class quality, and world-class companies are all impossible without an aggressive world-class training effort.

Bren's professional background has uniquely contributed to his insight, understanding, and implementation of world-class training. He has helped international companies become more globally competitive for over a decade. He has lived and worked in the United Kingdom, Belgium, France, and Greece.

I cannot refrain from feeling satisfaction that Bren took my courses in organizational leadership at Purdue University and that I have had the pleasure of working with him professionally over a period of years. The applications, examples, and comments he provides in this book will be especially appreciated by his readers.

Jim L. Windle, Ph.D.
Professor
Organizational Leadership
Purdue University
West Lafayette, Indiana

Contents

Introduction

Globalization is having an effect on everything, *literally everything*. Business executives say they know this and that they understand this fact. Yet most corporations still look and behave as they did five, 10, or 15 years ago. It seems incredible that organizational behavior is seriously lagging behind organizational rhetoric, and human development trails well behind technological development.

Kenichi Ohmae, in his recent book, *The Borderless World*, might give some readers the impression that fundamentally globalization means homogenization, a growing commonality across markets and cultures. On one level, and in particular industries, this may be true to some extent. However, the coinciding reality is that markets are splintering and becoming more and more specialized within the context of each existing market and culture. Overall, it is my view that business is definitely becoming more complex and global in scope by necessity. The point is that to be successful beyond the 90s, virtually all companies will have to "think globally and act locally." The ability to span the globe and serve many diverse market niches is now a possibility for small- and medium-size businesses via information technology and telecommunications. More than that, it is a necessity to stay competitive. The game has changed for even the largest multinational corporations.

Among all this change is a new imperative for most American managers — the need to become multicultural and multilingual. Business people cannot operate effectively (regardless of what some longtime jetsetters might say) on a global basis, in the new global context of business, without some major regauging of mindset, skills, and knowledge. There should be intimate knowledge of the culture, history, politics, economics, and commerce of every customer group your company serves and every competitor with whom you compete. You cannot understand your customers or provide real value and satisfaction without it. You cannot develop successful growth strategies without it.

Any old notions about the limitations and purpose or power of training and communications processes is no longer valid. Globalization is shoving us, all of us, into the unknown, into a new century. In this new age, past success is almost a liability. Crucial to future business success will be observations of the cultural norms of the organizational configurations and integration of training and executive development with strategic planning.

For the past decade or so I have helped corporations rethink the implications and the opportunities of globalization. In that time I have discovered the following:

- Agile thinkers with global skills who can transform their entire organization (what I refer to as world-class leaders) will be necessary for corporations to be responsive and world-class.

- The key to capturing and serving global markets is to install continual global learning at the heart of the organization. Until such a process is put into place, a competitive vacuum will continue to be created at the center of our paralyzed enterprises. The cracks and tarnishes on the surface will lead to final disintegration of what could have been vital and successful business organisms.

- The global window is already beginning to shut on many. For your company the window may be two, or perhaps fourteen months. If you are lucky, maybe three years. Every day is precious. Somebody in your organization needs to take action now. What are **you** and your management team going to do?

Chapter 1

The World-Class Challenge

1

The World-Class Challenge

*"Changing environmental forces and industry
characteristics are now forcing companies to
broaden their international strategic focus,
to recognize that competitive viability now
requires global efficiency, multinational flexibility,
and world-wide learning — all at the same time."*
— Bartlett & Ghoshal

The future hinges on people and technology and the innovative management of both. This is the world-class challenge! How can executives strategically employ people, ideas, technology, and money to create a whole new world of market niches and industries? The challenge that faces us all is nothing less than shaping a totally new world. Companies can no longer simply hold their ground in a mature domestic market or hold to any narrowly-defined traditional market position and expect to survive in the next century. Old mindsets must be shattered and old definitions must be destroyed. Forget the status quo with which most of us are so comfortable! If a future exists for you as a leader, follower, or corporate entity, it will only be because you invest in people strategically to help you compete in global markets.

Virtually all companies, regardless of size, are facing the new global reality. Competitive strategies can no longer be framed only in a domestic or local context.

Global influences will leave no industry untouched. With global telecommunications and international trade causing unbridled global financial flow, traditional boundaries have become virtually invisible and old competitive profiles irrelevant. As free world trade increases, the flow of money, people, products, and services rush at amazing speed in all directions. There are new rules and new competitors to contend with, and both are in every market — always changing. There is simply no escape. Companies, intent on surviving, must find a comprehensive way of dealing with these new world realities. As Howard V. Perlmutter of the Wharton Business School says, "There is no place to hide!"

Creating The Future

A good friend of mine used to respond sarcastically to radical social changes by remarking, "Is nothing sacred?" Looking around at all the incredible changes of the past decade, one might ask this same question. Nothing is standing still in the realm of business; everything deserves questioning and reassessment. If looked at properly, this new era of change can be seen as exciting and challenging.

Stanley Davis in his book *Future Perfect*, shares his vantage point about change and organizations' perceptions of change. "Organizations can do no better than catch up with the present, and there is a 'Catch 22' to catching up; when you get there, 'there' isn't there anymore. The name of the game, managerially and organizationally, is to catch up as quickly as possible." While this description accurately reflects the pace and complexity of the business world today, I don't completely agree with Davis' view that what organizations must do is "catch up." The organizations that are going to be the real winners are those who actually "create" the future. Often those corporations that do this will be the ones to go into a new niche first or to create demand in risking newly-opened markets. Alan Kay, early fellow at Apple Computer said, **"The best way to prepare for the future is to invent it."** This saying should be etched in gold over the entrance of every business today. Ten years ago it might have sounded arrogant and brash. Today it is a simple fact. If your company is not helping to boldly forge a new set of markets, it is going to be left out in the cold.

Self-Adjusting For Continuous Improvement

Organizations all over the world, regardless of industry or size, need to establish a philosophy that includes self-adjustment, or self-reformation. In order to self-adjust, organizations will have to ensure that continuous learning and improvement takes place. These organizations should understand thoroughly what is required by the customers in their markets and make certain that their organizations are committed to meet those needs better than all others. Again, many organizations are talking about this; few have been able to do much about it. The challenge is to engage people, technology, information, and other resources to fashion an ever-changing, value-adding process to create a future that ensures the organization has advantages over the competition literally anywhere in the world.

The Challenge Of A New Europe

While there are many changing markets to learn about, a unified Europe, representing a potential market larger than the U.S., is definitely worth studying. For instance, a rapidly-changing high tech information technology sector in Europe is entering a period of accelerated market-driven change. At the same time a new industrial framework is being forged as part of the unification process. Companies such as ABB, Siemens, Philips, Bull, ICL, and Thomson are influencing this framework and related change processes. Monetary, cultural, and standardization issues will play a crucial role in this complex unification. "Companies missing out on initial guidelines and policy may be at a real disadvantage later as the European market galvanizes. Opportunities do exist in this attractive market, but firms competing in Europe must respect the "new rules" of the game that are now being set. Robert Dalziel, AT&T executive, has commented that 1992 is a clear opportunity for non-EC firms. "But unless those firms are willing to transform themselves into EC firms, in every sense, I doubt they will have success."

Telecommunications firms across Europe and beyond are scrambling to get a piece of the action, both of a larger Europe and a newly-opened Eastern Europe. British Telecom (BT) and Cable & Wireless have done some aggressive repositioning in Europe and the U.S. AT&T, Alcatel, Italtel, Siemens, and Motorola have all thrown their hats in the ring. Motorola just built a sizeable plant in Scotland to produce cellular equipment, formed a strategic alliance with Alp Electric in Switzerland, and already has manufacturing facilities in Great Britain and Germany.

M. J. Monteiro, Vice President of 3M's International Operations, has this view of the changing European economic landscape: "After 1992, Europe will be a very different kind of market .... It will be characterized by fewer but stronger competitors .... lower prices and stiffer competition ...."

If you talk to many Euro-executives, they will tell you that market restructuring will probably be nowhere near complete by January 1993. They will also tell you that many small and medium-size companies have not yet focused market opportunities in Europe and do not yet have medium or long-term European business strategies. There is still some time to begin positioning for this emerging mega market.

The Challenge Of The Pacific Rim

Besides the emerging free market opportunities of a unified Europe, a new Eastern Europe and the former Soviet Union, there are many long- and near-term business prospects in Singapore, Thailand, China, India, Hong Kong, Korea, Philippines, Malaysia, Indonesia, Taiwan, Japan, and Australia. Most of the world's future growth will take place in this region. Japanese corporations have spun an incredible "net" of ventures, operations, and investment in their regional neighborhood. What should your organization be doing in these areas? How could it capitalize? What needs to happen for such new business initiatives to be implemented rapidly and effectively? What kind of "training effort" is going to be required to support successful ventures there?

Global Competitive Priorities

According to a Boston University study conducted in 1988, key global competitive priorities today include:

- Consistently high quality

- High performance products/value-added services

- Low prices

- Dependable deliveries

- Rapid design change

- After sales/service/rapid volume changes

What is your company doing in relation to each of these priorities? Are they **really** operating priorities?

Organizations must pay attention to these kind of global operating priorities. Speeches by top executives about global change are not enough. The systems they lead must meaningfully respond to these realities, and executives must decide how these systems are going to change because of them. It is critical that organizations find innovative ways of internalizing lessons learned from the outside world. Changes taking place outside organizations must be reflected in the design/redesign of all internal processes, ideas, systems, policies, and skills (not just the typical no-brainer restructuring that has littered the corporate countryside in the U.S. over the past decade or so). A major rethinking is long overdue for many companies. Some need to redefine their view of the world, their vision for their businesses, and their products and services.

Did you know that the Japanese spend three to four times that of most of their Western counterparts per employee on training? In Japan continuing education is part of the work process, absorbing on the average eight hours per week for every employee, with half on company time and the other half on employees' time. Most companies are not contemplating spending anywhere near the amount of dollars necessary to become globally competitive. As one Japanese government official said in the 1980s, "We have studied. **We are prepared.** Now we are ready." There are many corporations today that cannot honestly say this.

See Global/Be Mobile!

Some advice: Don't wait until domestic markets are saturated before going abroad with your marketing efforts. Go wherever the best opportunities are! Doug Fulmer, international marketing consultant, says a company's global business potential far outstrips total current domestic revenues. He notes that companies such as Dow, IBM, Black & Decker, and Mitsubishi have non-domestic based revenues of over 40 percent. It's definitely worth the investment. There are many new market niches where your company can compete. Find them and equip your employees to face the challenge!

In December of 1989 in Croton-on-the-Hudson, New York, Jack Welch, chairman of GE, made his central message for the 1990s and beyond known to his top 100 executives: spread the gospel of productivity throughout the 271,000 person organization, and "give everyone the necessary tools." While this event by itself guarantees little, it at least sets a clear tone. Equipping employees for competitiveness is the single most important investment companies can make today. This equipping cannot be spotty or half-planned. It must be an integral part of a larger orchestrated change strategy and should be woven into the very cultural fabric of the organization. Corporate strategy without a major training component is doomed to fail in the long run (forget about this quarter and next and begin imagining what the world could look like five, 10, or 15 years from now — it will be here before you know it.)

In the 1990s and twenty-first century, the major issue in corporations of all sizes around the world will be to attain and sustain world-class performance. Corporations will not become world-class providers of quality services without continually learning and improving. It is just that simple. And that learning must be world-class in both quality and focus.

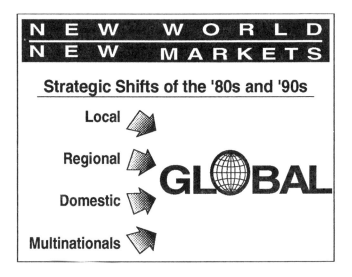

In the next chapter we will discuss how a training process is a vital requirement for success in global markets.

Chapter 2

World-Class Training —
Meeting The Challenge

2

World-Class Training — Meeting The Challenge

"Institute a vigorous program of education
and self-improvement."
— W. Edwards Deming

Today training is not an "It's nice to have, but" issue. It is strictly a competitive issue. Companies that don't aggressively equip all their employees to compete in today's globalized markets will not remain viable for very long. While this fact may have occurred to you long before this, perhaps how to prepare and train a corporation for these markets has evaded you so far.

World-Class Tip

To compete successfully in the fully globalized and differentiated markets of the twenty-first century, corporations will have to begin developing globally-oriented and skilled employees today.

Training Should Be Value-Producing

My fundamental premise is that training should be designed and used as the single greatest value-producing process inside any enterprise. Training should no longer be viewed as something nice to do, something to placate professionals, or a drain in human productivity. It should be considered and designed to be the ultimate value-producing process for the organization.

It happens every week somewhere. Top executives launch a new initiative for change, a fashionable program of some sort, usually concocted by a joint effort between corporate communications and human resource executives. They launch it in the name of enlightenment and competitiveness, and still no transformation takes place — nothing seems to really work in changing that core status quo. Few executives in organizational development training, or otherwise, really know how to go about reconditioning whole organizational systems. Many have tried and failed. This makes each new try that much harder. There is a right way, albeit complex, and it always involves training. Walk into many training departments, and you will find that much of what is occurring is a repackaging of what has been happening in training for the last 10-20 years. This should be disturbing to someone! Even those companies who see themselves as too small to have a training function should reassess the need for an ongoing training process that will help them achieve competitive advantage in market niches over the long haul.

Training efforts have to change radically, and soon. Traditional approaches have to go. Corporations can no longer afford to simply provide "smorgasbord training." Training today must be strategic in every respect, and must be global in scope. Without these two fundamental elements, training becomes little more than an organizational placebo.

Training provides a legitimate pretext and a concrete mechanism for implementing and sustaining change. Most of us know how often "OD projects" and fad programs fail to yield lasting results. An ongoing, strategic training process integrated into a larger organizational game plan can really stimulate and sustain important change. Training must become the change vehicle, the single most important lever in the change process.

A Revolutionary Learning Process

While there is almost no way to keep up with all the incredible changes taking place across the globe, there is a process which can help organizations of all types focus strategically and stay in synch with the globalized markets they serve. Most importantly, this revolutionary learning process provides an aggressive employee-equipping method that will help to ensure competitiveness globally in the long-term. This learning process I call world-class training.

World-class training is a comprehensive way of successfully managing necessary organizational change, which is constant. Strategies evolve at the speed of light (hopefully). Implementation of these strategies must keep pace somehow. Companies cannot afford to lag behind while competitors capitalize on timing and positioning. World-class training is a way to orchestrate change through an organizational learning process that helps employees sense strategic shifts in the outside world. With this knowledge employees can respond with the necessary changes that enable the organization to achieve and/or maintain competitive advantage.

Characteristics Of World-Class Training

In all world-class training, the following characteristics are essential:

- **A strong and all-pervasive global focus rather than a national, regional, or local one.** This alone has tremendous implications for most organizations. A few multinational firms have made efforts to establish a global focus, but many of these commendable attempts need major revamping. As GE's Jack Welch has proclaimed, "Globalization is no longer an objective, but an imperative." Most companies, however, are doing very little to develop global training. Cultural ethnocentricity often obscures any perceived need to do so. This is true in the United States in particular.

Training that has this kind of international focus must not be saved just for executives, fast trackers, and professional jetsetters. It is absolutely imperative that all of it, including the cross-cultural and foreign language training, be provided to interested employees system-wide. Administrative, support, finance, and technical employees need to have the same (or better) understanding and appreciation of global issues as executives have.

Knowledge and skills that allow employees to better understand their globalized customer bases and their global competitors must be systematically and broadly developed throughout an organization. Of course, if an organization has no desire to exist in the twenty-first century, then world-class training isn't necessary. Basically, an organization has between 5 and 10 years to get into this ongoing adaptive process. Periodic and painful restructurings are old school.

- **Training that is flexible and self-adapting.** Training changes or varies its content and media as required by world events and strategic shifts. It becomes a central mechanism for assimilating change organization-wide. Its own design and focus must constantly reflect the ever-changing reality of global customers and competitors. Because of this characteristic, it is pivotal in keeping the organization agile and responsive. This, as you know, is critical.

- **A focused and integrated learning process.** This process should be based on new-world business strategies and skills. It must incorporate the knowledge, skills, and communication systems that will keep the employees up-to-date with the world.

- **Many disciplines under an organizational development framework. Typical programs include:**
    - Global courses and briefings
    - Cross-cultural skills training
    - Innovative leadership, executive development, amd learning processes
    - Professional development forums
    - Technical skills courses strategically relevant to the business
    - PC skills programs
    - Customer service skills training
    - Team process and continuous improvement skills training

- **A philosophy that encourages learning in many forms.** This philosophy must be a dominant feature of the organizational culture.

- **Training that is of strategic value to the organization.** Training is more than just skill-building; it includes learning new perspectives, new styles of thinking, new behaviors, new information, and new forums for cross-boundary discussion of critical organizational issues.

  It is important that the implementation and management of the training process be strategic in the political sense. The political realities of the organization must be considered. This may be one of the most important factors in implementation and management of world-class training, and yet there is no exact recipe for doing this in all organizations. World-class training, as you might guess, must be tailored completely to each organization. It is an intuitive and consultative project of some magnitude.

- **Training that is customer-focused.** Charles Moritz (CEO Dun & Bradstreet) has said, "Customer focus is the basic attitude that produces change.... As successful companies navigate change, I believe that customer focus is the star to steer by."

  When you have mastered a customer focus, the rest will happen with basic, steady engineering. Don't begin investing your company's resources until you have resolved this basic issue. Where, how, and to whom are you in the best position to provide value? Once you've honestly answered these strategic questions, then you can begin customer-focused training.

Organizations must be both customer-focused and strategic in their actions. Tremendous amounts of energy have to be concentrated on the customer to yield the highest results. All decision-making and planning must make the customer central. Every action taken, every policy or procedure established, every new initiative implemented must be in the ultimate best interest of the customer, if the payback is to be lasting. People throughout the organization need to learn and share this common value for customer focus. It should begin with the behaviors of key executives and leaders at all levels, and it must be reinforced daily.

• **Training that is continuously employed to achieve competitive advantage**. To meet this criteria, training must be constantly redesigned to reflect the thinking and behaviors it is striving to convey to the organization. (If your training functions are structured and function as they did 10-15 years ago, the situation has to be remedied quickly for the rest of the organization to reach its full potential.)

There really are no "success stories" in any absolute sense. As Tom Peters will readily tell you, "excellent companies" last year aren't necessarily excellent today. The world has become unpredictably dynamic.

Executives and managers of all industries must learn to learn continuously, to intuit, to envision at high speed, and to adapt to and make sense of pervasive ambiguity.

- **Training administrative processes, courses, seminars, and forums that directly contribute to the successful implementation of business strategies for targeted markets.**

- **Training that fully captures the imagination of all potential internal customers.** To do this, the training must be thoroughly and artfully marketed and woven into the political and cultural fabric of the organization. Everyone must be completely sold on the training framework and packaging that is developed. It must be absolutely fitting for an organization in a given window of time. It must also include methods to naturally invest people personally and professionally.

It makes little difference which company you are working for. Nothing is guaranteed. The strongest strategic position can evaporate in a month in the new world marketplace. Only the people in the organization can determine the continuing viability of the enterprise. What is in their hearts and minds will decide the fate of the corporation. One or two people can develop visions and strategies, but it take many totally committed people to convert those images and strategies into reality.

World-Class Employees

If you employ world-class training in your organization, you will have employees who:

- Are fluent in languages, such as Japanese, Russian, Spanish, German, French, Italian, Portuguese, Korean, Hungarian, Czech, Polish, Swahili, and Chinese.

- Understand how the European Community works.

- Have lived abroad for an extended period.

- Have mastered the art of cross-cultural negotiation.

- Are extremely customer-focused.

- Understand the importance of continuous improvement.

- Are challenged and excited about coming to work everyday.

- Are PC literate.

- Really understand international economics and finance.

- Can articulate the corporate global vision.

- Have a deep appreciation of other cultures.

- Can see the future as something other than just an extension of the past.

- Can explain the company's strategic strengths in non-domestic markets.

- Have intimate knowledge of process redesign, total quality, statistical process control, real-time manufacturing, and value-added selling.

Unless your organization is just extremely rare, there is probably much preparing and equipping to be done. World-class organizations are filled with people who possess these competencies. If your company is calling itself world-class, and yet is not aggressively addressing how to equip its employees, you are just kidding yourself. Every organization interested in remaining viable long-term should stop and consider the kind of major investment in people it is going to require. You literally should be "in training" for the business Olympics and your organization filled with Olympic hopefuls. If you don't train them properly, you are going to lose. It is just that simple.

Essentially, what I am suggesting is that world-class training is not just another fad notion that should be pursued to keep up with the "Corporate Joneses," but rather a revolutionary and pragmatic process by which organizations can keep themselves competitive into the twenty-first century.

The chapters that follow provide information about key ingredients of the world-class training process in relation to:

- An organization's leaders — Chapter 3: World-Class Leadership

- An organization's employees — Chapter 4: Gold-Collar Employees

- Cross-cultural training — Chapter 5: The Cross-Cultural Maze

- Communicating an organization's vision — Chapter 6: Big Picture Training

- Design of training — Chapter 7: A Practical Blueprint

Chapter 3

World-Class Leadership

3

World-Class Leadership

*"Challenging conventional wisdom is crucial to
restoring a company's competitive edge."*
Robert Galvin, former Chairman, Motorola

Large corporations can't remain leaders by trying to
"keep up" with the competition. They must actively work
to develop leaders and professionals who will be effective
in the world of the next century. If bold thinking and
innovative training are not employed to prepare corporate
leaders for the future, competitive disadvantage will be the
result. The companies who take a daring and innovative
lead will simply dominate any market they focus on. New-
world thinking and new-world skills are needed right now,
not just five or 10 years from now.

All leadership is developed through an active, dynamic
learning process. There are no automatic leaders. The
myth of the "born leader" has done irreparable damage to
many corporations worldwide. The fact is, no human
being becomes a great leader without rigorous preparation
and usually some kind of mentoring by someone who cares
and is able to inspire. Organizations that need leadership
must actively stimulate and guide the learning process to
create world-class leaders.

Two Levels Of Leadership

World-class leadership can occur on both the individual and the corporate level. The two go together — you can't have one without the other. World-class leaders set the tone in world-class organizations. Let's take a look at the organizations that are leading the way and attaining world-class status.

Characteristics Of Organizations That Are Leaders

What characterizes organizations that are providing world-class leadership? Tom Peters, in his 1987 book, *Thriving on Chaos*, identified five keys to world-class leadership:

1) An obsession with responsiveness to customers.

2) Constant innovation in all areas of the firm.

3) Partnership, the wholesale participation of and gainsharing with all people connected with the organization.

4) Leadership that loves change (instead of fighting it) and instills and shares an inspiring vision.

5) Control by means of simple support systems aimed at measuring the "right stuff" for today's environment.

Organizational Leaders

There are perhaps a hundred or so corporations worldwide that can truly be said to be world-class. The rest are just pretending — blowing smoke! Some of the companies that provide world-class leadership are: Subaru, Isuzu, Armstrong, AMP, Fujitsu, NTT, Millipore, Motorola, Honda, Lilly & Co., British Telecom, Mitsubishi, Ericsson, Toyota, Daimler-Benz, Federal Express, Philips, Disney, Matsushita, Microsoft, NEC, Royal Bank of Canada, and Sony. Although not perfect, these organizations have been able to demonstrate leadership in the global marketplace, each in their own strategic niches.

One example of world-class leadership is ICI, the "supertanker" of global chemical companies. During the late 1980s, ICI made strategic shifts to a world-class status. If you drive down I-95 between Wilmington, Delaware and Baltimore, Maryland in the U.S., you will see ICI's "world-class" motto on the wall of their large U.S. pharmaceutical production facility. ICI has became a more accessible, competitive, and responsive company under the leadership of Denys Henderson and Sir John Harvey-Jones. Although the company has had an extremely aggressive acquisition strategy, several key organizational changes have been made. There has been not only a shift in product mix and geographic positioning but also organizational changes to match. ICI has moved from "dull" to "exciting" as it has penetrated Europe and North America and other markets. As Sir John Harvey-Jones retired in 1987, he commented, "We've got our pride back at ICI. We're now knocking spots off the international competition."

ICI's use of the term **world-class** in their advertising and in connection with their logo has great significance. They are clearly communicating to the world that their name represents this "positioning" concept. If earnest about this desire to be world-class, ICI stands to achieve all its strategic operating objectives and become the major player in many global chemical, paint, pharmaceutical, and biotech markets. The key will be what ICI does internally to assure that the reality continues to match the claim. What may be required is a rethinking of the leadership process.

WORLD-CLASS TIP

World-class leadership has less to do with earnings per share or profit before tax and more to do with envisioning, creating, value-adding, positioning, seeding, networking, intrapreneuring, entrepreneuring, and caring.

Millipore Corporation is another example of a company that is attaining world-class status. Small in size by some standards, Millipore is a successful global corporation that is nurturing the global aspect of the enterprise using many different vehicles, including training and communication.

A number of factors set Millipore apart as a global organization.

- Filling top jobs almost exclusively with people who have "global profiles" makes a major difference.

- Regular management and sales meetings are held in which people from all over the globe meet to exchange information and communicate openly about important business issues.

- A worldwide newsletter features stories and articles from around the world to help give the company a truly global orientation and identity.

- Cross-functional and cross-boundary fertilization is encouraged, especially among the top management group, whose members are located in several different countries.

- A European, an Asian, and a U.S. council have been created to address global issues on a regular basis. The councils have close ties with each other and the corporation's executive committee.

This kind of world-class management process is fairly rare, and seeing a small firm taking such a leadership role in the global marketplace is a good sign. Other organizations — large and small — may soon emerge that will take a similar leadership position. Indeed, Michael Bonsignore, COO of Honeywell, said in *Industry Week* that successful global companies will "see global business as a global enterprise, balance where and how, stay for the long haul, take a worldwide view, organize as a global enterprise, and manage people on a global basis." This is exceptional advice and is becoming widely accepted. It requires a totally new mindset about business.

Our third example of a world-class leader is based in Canada. The Royal Bank of Canada is the fourth largest bank in North America with 55,000 employees in over 40 countries. It is currently in the process of major organizational redesign, although it is not being called that. The Royal Bank is simply doing what it sees as essential to its future global success. It is actively involving employees in deciding how work processes are organized and performed.

Warren Bull, former senior vice president of corporate planning and productivity for the bank, reflects on the advice of Dartmouth professor Brian Quinn. Quinn suggested that "overhead services which are not world-class should be outsourced to world-class suppliers." The idea is that this would increase quality, flexibility, responsiveness, and accountability. Peter Drucker calls this "the unbundling of our corporations."

Bull points out that "there is much unlearning to do from the bad habits and thinking conditioned by the 1960s and 1970s. He says that "knowledge gained over the last three decades is virtually worthless," and that executives and employees alike need to learn a fresh new way of thinking about what successful business is all about. He continues his striking observation by noting that "in the 1990s there will be no way to protect the status quo. The forces of globalization will not allow it. Leaders will be repositioning their enterprises for a world market like we've never seen...all conventional wisdom is out the window."

There are five major organizational shifts Bull believes must happen during the 90s:

1. Management hierarchy must collapse.

2. Top management and customer management must collaborate closely as a major force for change.

3. Organizational networking must be promoted.

4. People will come *first*.

5. Work and contribution must be revalued.

The dynamic trek upon which the Royal Bank has embarked is a form of world-class training: the blending of organizational change, global learning, and competitive "regauging" involving all employees. Every firm's reaction to globalization is going to be somewhat different. The key is translating global reality into organizational reality. All-encompassing fluid change external to the organization warrants all-encompassing and fluid change internally. This seems to be something this world-class leader has fully grasped.

Now let's look at the other side of the leadership coin. Remember, you can't have world-class leadership without world-class leaders.

Characteristics Of The Individual Leader—The Global Profile

Today there is an incredible shortage of effective leaders in our world, at a time when leadership is most crucial. My strong belief is that the top priority of corporations, schools, and other organizations should be to develop world-class leaders. The need is urgent. There can be no more waiting for leaders with global profiles to magically appear!

What makes these "global profiles" different? What makes a leader world-class? What skills, abilities, and experience set top managers apart from more traditional domestic managers?

My research suggests that the following characteristics are major differentiators of a world-class leader:

- The ability to see "the possibilities" globally—to be a visionary

- A strategic mindset

- An ability to keep pace with rapid change

- An openness to learning reflected in a deep curiosity about people and the world

- An innovative spirit

- The ability to speak several languages fluently

- An understanding of international markets and global finance

- An understanding of organizational development

- The ability to inspire followers with diverse backgrounds

- A tolerance of ambiguity, making sense out of confusion

- Excellent listening and observation skills

- The ability to manage conflict

- The ability to negotiate

- The ability to solve problems

- A deep understanding of cross-cultural issues

- Flexibility

- Decisiveness

- Personal integrity

What is the message for managers around the world? If there is a single message, it is this: **Develop a global mindset or lose your position of leadership.** The message may sound strong, but it needs to. Global managers are moving the world forward in revolutionary jolts. Leaders without a clear global view and the facility to understand new global realities will be severely limited in their influence and effectiveness. As Bill McGowen, founder of MCI, said on many occasions, "The future is global." Having a global view is the pivotal point for successful corporations of tomorrow.

WORLD-CLASS TIP

World-class leadership hinges on visionary leaders who can see all the possibilities of emerging global markets.

Individual Leaders

There may be hundreds or thousands of managers worldwide who would qualify as world-class leaders— who have a global profile. Some who measure up against the stiffest criteria that is emerging for the "global leader" are Percy Barnevik of ASEA Brown Boveri, Marc Moret of Sandoz, Wisse Dekker of Philips, George Fisher of Motorola, Frank Popoff of Dow, Denys Henderson of ICI, and Irimajiri of Honda. More world-class leaders include

Jan Timmer of N.V. Philips, Christian Zetterberg of Volvo, and Tadashi Kume of Honda.

Another individual with a global profile is Bob Postlethwait, now vice president of international for Eli Lilly & Co. in London. Bob lived for a number of years in Italy, Argentina, and Brazil. He has an excellent understanding of these cultures and is fluent in several languages. Without this kind of knowledge, experience, and understanding, world-class leaders will not emerge. There are too few now — the result of a narrow view of international training and development. This global profile is an important development because it represents an idea that must be addressed by corporate training and education. Lilly provides a good example of how global leader development can be done with successful business results.

WORLD-CLASS TIP

The new profile of a world-class leader is someone with international background, skills, and mindset. World-class leaders set the tone in organizations. They are bold, visionary, and intuitive. They are listeners and synthesizers who know how to enlist and inspire. Moreover, they understand the world, its peoples, languages, cultures, politics, economics, and history. Fill your top jobs primarily with those global, world-class executives.

A subset of this global profile is the Euro-executive. What experience, behaviors, knowledge, insights, perspectives, and skills are required of an effective manager in the Europe of tomorrow? Let's take a closer look at a few examples.

Apple Computer invested in just such a profile. The former president of Apple Products, charismatic Frenchman Jean-Louis Gasse, not only helped to establish Apple France but also was responsible for the introduction of the incredibly popular Mac SE and modular Mac II line. Loved by Apple employees and known as a visionary leader, Monsieur Gasse reflects this new global profile.

Soren Olsson, the new president of Apple Europe, is a brand of this new profile, also. The forty-four-year-old executive has management experience bridging Sweden, Norway, Denmark, Finland, Iceland, Germany, Austria, and Eastern European countries. Now he is getting exposure to additional markets in Europe, Africa, and the Middle East. He speaks several languages fluently and has experience in operations and marketing. Apple has done similarly in Asia and is seeing the positive results, especially in Japan.

Tom Brindisi, Michael Illich, and Ken Walsh, international search executives, all spend much of their time searching for the "global profile" for global corporations. They agree that the development of such a profile within corporations is probably the most vital business issue of this decade.

Bruce Crockett, CEO of COMSAT, is a fast-moving profile. Always on the go around the globe, he and his general managers move decisively to shift a very traditional, stable business into high gear in the ferocious world telecommunications marketplace. Previously at COMSAT the missing pieces to the change puzzle had included corporate culture, leadership, and people development.

Another world-class leader, Frank Popoff, the CEO of Dow Chemical, has been deeply involved in global markets for many years. His multilingual, multicultural profile gives him keen insight and advantage where the global arena is concerned. He told me he first became involved in international business in Europe in the 1960s. From the very beginning he said Dow tried to "minimize capital investment but maximize its investment in people." He believes the company has done well on a global basis not because of large sums of capital being expended but because of "first class people" running "first class facilities."

Today, half of all Dow's business is non-domestic. This didn't happen overnight. "Markets can be won by exports, but not held by exports," says Dow's chief executive. Because of its investment strategy and attention to its human resources worldwide, it is well-positioned in the European Community among other markets, such as Japan. He comments about seemingly tough markets to crack like Japan, "Some companies complain — others just find a way to do it!"

One way Dow stays competitively agile is through constant appraisal of organizational capabilities and market opportunities. Where there are industry dilemmas or market opportunities, the question is, "What can we do about it...or with it?" It is this kind of openness to change and investment in people that will make or break many companies in the 90s. Maybe some crucial lessons can be learned from the leadership of Frank Popoff and the successes of Dow.

One point that can't be missed about global profiles is that, as a group, they are multicultural. ASEA Brown Boveri's executive group is made up of mostly Swedish, Swiss, and German executives. Twenty of Dow's top executives have global experience. Forty percent of ICI's top 170 executives are not British (five nationalities are represented). The majority of Johnson & Johnson's key executives worldwide are not Americans. One third of CPC International's officers are foreign nationals. Procter & Gamble has appointed its international operations chief to be its new CEO. At Hewlett-Packard, five of 25 officers are **not** U.S. citizens, and all offshore units are managed locally. Honda's Irimiajiri got the top job "back home" because of his U.S. experience, his "global profile."

Let me give you a profile of a "global" executive, and see if you can guess what his nationality is. He resides in the state of Massachusetts in the U. S. He took a sabbatical to earn a master's in electrical engineering from the University of Illinois. He speaks faster than most New York cabbies and boasts a golf handicap of 20. He is chairman of a $1 billion company with 2,600 employees. What do you think? This description is derived from the bio of Dr. Hisao Kanai of NEC Technologies, Inc.

We live in a globalized world made up of "global managers." These are people who have developed their language abilities and cross-cultural skills to the degree that you can't identify them as "foreigners" until you hear their name (perhaps) or company information. More and more global managers will be found across all cultures as globalization is fully realized.

World-class corporations generally are developing multi-cultural management teams. What these leaders have in common and whether they operate in world-class ways will be informative to us. However, no matter how instructive examples of "world-class" companies or managers and executives may be, the key is to look more at principles of change that are the foundation for successful behavior in an integrated world. Even the best examples of multinational management may fail as time unfolds. Only the principles can be trusted. The principles that must be followed for world-class leadership to flourish are:

- Sense of vision/mission

- Speed

- Global perspective

- Responsiveness

- Value

- Quality

- Continuous improvement

- Teamwork

- Flexibility

- Adaptability

- Confidence

- Excitement for the future

- Continual learning

- Cross-cultural connection

Any organization striving to become world-class needs to consider these principles when developing a customized profile for its world-class leaders.

Let's take a closer look at three of these principles: sense of vision (visionary leadership), speed (keeping pace with rapid change), and a global perspective (a new mindset).

Visionary Leadership

One thing that keeps surfacing in my discussions and research is the difference between what world-class leaders and traditional leaders see as important. Probably the most noticeable difference is a world-class leader's ability to deal effectively with fundamental issues of the business at an intuitive level. World-class leaders prefer to play with an ever-changing vision rather than concentrating on numbers. Also important is the desire and ability to share that vision with people in such a way that they are challenged, excited, and fully committed to it.

WORLD-CLASS TIP

The faster the world moves into the future, the more strategic and intuitive an organization and its leaders must become.

Japanese companies like Honda and Toyota have executed an incredible vision in the global marketplace. Honda has a very clear, long-term vision of what is going to happen in U.S. markets. They have developed a comprehensive five-step strategy that all employees understand and is the basis for all training activities.

World-class leadership is not just a characteristic of multinational corporations of the 1960s, 1970s, and 1980s. It is a new brand of leadership for the 1990s and the next century for all companies—customer-focused and people-driven. It hinges on visionary leaders who can imagine the world configured in a radically different way and can see all the possibilities of globalized economies and their emerging markets. It is a leadership not of control but of commitment and one that is enlightened and caring. The new global corporate revolution will be led by real people (not back room committees) and will be carried out by highly skilled, well-informed, networked teams of high-performance individuals. Harness this force, and capture major world markets yet unborn. Today turns into tomorrow rapidly. There is no waiting. World-class leaders know this best.

Keeping Pace With Rapid Change
"Those who learn from life and understand the need for change don't need to be afraid." Jack Hannon, vice president of COMSAT, shared this potent Gorbachev statement in an executive off-site retreat in 1989. The point he was making was that although change is risky and a little scary or uncomfortable, it is crucial to the competitive process. The message to all managers today is that there is no secure place, no protection from constant and merciless change.

WORLD-CLASS TIP
There is no innovation, no learning, no competitive spirit where change is avoided and foot dragging is allowed.

In his book, *The New Realities*, Peter Drucker remarks, "The knowledge society also requires all its members to learn how to learn. It is the very nature of knowledge that it changes fast." One of the key points made by Jack Bowsher in his 1989 book, *Educating America*, has to do with the undervaluing of the learning process and the lack of effective leadership. Bowsher states that "education will be the issue of the 1990's." What are we going to be learning about? Globalization, of course, among other things.

"If America is to regain its competitive edge, it will have to develop the less educated half of the work force, which — unlike money, managers, and technology — is the only ingredient for economic development that cannot be easily moved almost anywhere in the world," comments Lester Thurow, dean of the Sloan School of Management at MIT. Business leaders have been saying for years that people are our most important asset. Now they must demonstrate it. As Bob Cowie, senior vice president of Dana Corporation, says, "It's not what top management says, it's what it does that counts." Remember — deeds, not words.

Tom Peters emphasizes in *Thriving on Chaos* that we are living in a world in which relative skill advantage (skill upgrading) will be the principal advantage. He says that without qualification CEO's have a massive challenge before them as they move into the twenty-first century. He offers this insight for today's top executives who are interested in being world-class leaders:

> We are now moving from an era where words such as detached, calculative, dispassionate, analytic, methodical were cherished into the new world

where words like fast, intuitive, hustling, caring, trusting, empathizing, cheerleading, skill building, mistake-making, and above all, fast-action taking (experimenting) will be honored.

Look at what is happening around the world in broad terms. There is virtually total technological connectivity around the globe. However, there is not a similar degree of human connectivity. Transformation, reformation, and total redefining of political, social, and economic systems are missing. Organizations need to ask questions regarding their own systems, such as: Is transformation, reformation, and redefining occurring within our organization? Are we transforming every process to fit the task at hand? Are new industries and markets being ignored for lack of guts and vision and imagination or because we simply haven't learned how to change quickly enough?

Breaking Out of Old Mindsets
The most important step for world-class leaders to take is to adopt a new mindset. The whole process of leadership and the development of people and organizations is being revolutionized. Corporations are struggling because external change is extremely fast and internal change is slow. Frustrations can run high just because of this single incongruity. The struggle that most organizations face today is in dealing with this discrepancy. What the customer demands has never been so out of whack with what the organization is willing to deliver. It is no wonder that bold companies, both those that are new and small and those that are large and adaptive, are building market share and new markets like never before.

Whether executives have a background in finance or legal or operations will not matter as much as how strong a global mindset and skillset they have. In her 1986 book, *International Dimensions of Organizational Behavior,* Nancy Adler, foremost expert in multinational management development, of McGill University, says of "globalized" managers:

> From their early time in the company, they're building up a level of knowledge, of awareness, and even more important, skill to be able to negotiate across different cultures, to be able to manage a group that has multicultural membership, to be able to 'read' the external environments in the various countries in which they operate. These are the types of skills—often discussed over time because they will be very critical for fast-track managers slated for company leadership.

The world-class training view goes one step further and suggests that **all** employees, if they are going to remain competitive in the global marketplace, need to have some of these same skills and awareness.

Many of the players entering the 1990s didn't even exist in the early 1970s. It seems just like yesterday, and yet the roster reads so differently. What should this fact tell us? The message should be clear: **Change your view of things and the way you operate, or be rooted out!** You need to stop clinging to a self-preservationist view, take a hard look at the real world, develop a global mindset, build the best teams to beat out the competition, strive for excellence, and be a bold risk taker.

WORLD-CLASS TIP
World-class leadership requires a capacity for organizational self-honesty.

The "golden parachute," self-preserving mindset of the 1970s and 1980s has now become one of the corporation's greatest liabilities. Corporate leaders who are incapable of actively serving and developing customer and employee relationships are literally of negative value to the organization. They are costing you money! Someone fulfilling a figurehead role in an aristocratic hierarchy is not in the company's best interest.

Corporate executives may find it difficult to break out of the self-preservation mode and shift to the common good and the long view. This shift, among others, is absolutely essential, however, for corporations to remain vital and productive forces in the new world economy. **Right now there is too much talk and not nearly enough action by key executives.** This shift in viewpoint is the ultimate test of leadership. Gutsy, comprehensive new strategies must be forged and executed in a fresh, collaborative style. The next few years will provide the window of opportunity to participate in the global game. All those who are holding back or sitting it out, or who are too slow to evaluate, invest, and adjust will certainly become extinct.

The hallmark of world-class leaders is the ability to continually readjust to meet the needs of rapidly changing situations. This ability requires an interactive style. This style is characterized by an openness and responsiveness to suggestions from others, and no personal need to be perfect. Leaders who are globally-minded place their highest value on people and their development and recognize the need to develop people skills by involving others in decision-making.

Another mindset that can cause complacency and diminished productivity in a corporate society is the blinding pride and parochialism resulting from success. Ian Valence, chairman of British Telecom, has said, "Success is a risky business. Within itself it causes the seeds of failure — complacency, ignorance, and a lightheaded arrogance." Valence and his BT management team are determined to capitalize on globalization. They are taking a fresh look and moving boldly on many fronts to implement the global vision.

WORLD-CLASS TIP
The next few years will provide a narrow window of opportunity for entrance into the global game.

My suggestion to you is that while there are seeds of failure within success, it is true, also, that the seeds for future success can be found in failings. Rather than looking at what other corporations are doing to become more competitive, we should recognize that we can improve. Once we have assessed our weaknesses and strengths, we will have to commit our energies and resources, educate our employees, and act upon our visions.

World-class leadership requires this capacity for organizational self-examination. In 1986 Nissan president Yukata Kume addressed a most difficult period by acknowledging, "This is a time of self-criticism to discover what is wrong with us." Not too many top executives seem to have this capacity or desire.

The Japanese view world markets as an opportunity to expand the demand for their products, develop their capabilities, and demonstrate responsiveness. The successes the Japanese have had suggest that, in order to be competitive, other countries will have to initiate actions quickly and move decisively. Those who procrastinate will lose the race.

Tom Peters states that our global marketplace has had a virtually immeasurable increase in the number of competitors producing top quality goods and services. In addition, the number of potential network partners with whom to form alliances to conquer a market has vastly increased. Worldwide markets are available to anyone of any size with goods or services of value. He also says there will be continued economic volatility and surprises of the sort we've witnessed for the last several years.

Many American executives have trouble breaking out of old mindsets and thinking globally. Robert Lepage, chairman, European Operations, Korn/Ferry International, wrote in a June 1990 article of *Europe Magazine:*

> Executives in the United States have more faith in long-term U.S. stability, than do their counterparts abroad....Despite several world-wide agents... American [executives] consistently discount the importance of...an international outlook, the impact of EC unification in 1992, and the value of foreign-language training. There is powerful evidence that the size and diversity of the American marketplace and its history of economic pre-eminence are blinding American CEO's to the demand for global business skills.

WORLD-CLASS TIP

World-class leaders know the importance of every employee learning to think globally and more strategically. Global thinking is, of course, the ultimate competitive edge.

Roger Milliken provides an example of a CEO who broke out of a mindset to restructure his company. In the 1980s, Milliken & Co. was a lot like any other U.S. corporate giant. Management told workers what to do and how to do it. Ideas for improvement flowed from the top. Then Roger Milliken read Phil Cosby's book, *Quality Is Free*. He began to understand that management, not labor, is responsible for the relatively poor quality of U.S. goods. He also realized that if the company didn't radically restructure, it might not survive. He said, "There was no way we could win the economic war without a totally new plan." Milliken decided to turn his company upside down. "He snatched power from management, found the problems, and then tried to solve them," says one manager. "But we empowered workers to take care of that. Perhaps the biggest change of all has been psychological...." "The secret is in asking workers what they think and showing them that you really care," Milliken says. Milliken's obsession with teamwork and employee involvement has served his company well. Over the past five years, the privately-owned firm has emerged as one of the USA's highest-quality manufacturers. U.S. President George Bush has referred to Milliken by saying the "company's management style is sheer twenty-first century."

Ghandi once stated, "The means must be pure for the ends to be pure." The reality that must register today is that executives cannot expect excellence to be produced by nonexcellent systems or processes. You cannot simply restructure, lop off a few hundred people, manipulate numbers, and expect to see long-term success. Quality results require comprehensive redesigning.

WORLD-CLASS TIP

Executives cannot expect excellence to be produced by less than excellent systems or processes. Build quality into your organization, even if it means rethinking and redesigning every system, every process, every procedure.

World-class products, world-class manufacturing, world-class quality, and world-class customer services are not labels companies can freely paste on inferior output and expect to compete in the global market. "World-class" is determined by individual customers around the world, not by superficial executives and high-powered advertising. Organizations have to strive to develop quality processes and the excellent people who will ensure excellent results over time. This kind of excellence comes only from commitment and respect; it cannot be mandated, negotiated, or coerced.

A global perspective will require boldness. Bold moves do winners make. Someone once said, "Make no small plans, for they have no power to stir your soul." Virtually every industry is being reshaped by the boldest competitors, the most adaptable companies, the best globally-tuned executives and professionals. As Michael Porter commented in his 1990 book, *Competitive Advantage of*

Nations, "Established leaders lose position if they stand still while industry structural change provides the opportunity for new firms to leapfrog to a new generation of products or process technology."

Ancient Chinese strategist and educator Sun Zu wrote in 500 B.C., "The king is only fond of words and cannot translate them into deeds." Similarly, many top executives of many corporations approach change by "wishing" for results or mandating results without thoroughly rethinking, redesigning, and retraining. As you might guess, wishing alone is not very productive. Somehow they lack a total understanding of the change in mindset that is required to provide world-class output.

Stop wasting time with perpetual people and paper shuffling that doesn't provide value to the customer! Direct your organization's energies into an aggressive, ongoing people-development process that produces new value to customers and continuous payback to the business. It sounds so simple, but it takes foresight and guts. It takes world-class leadership.

WORLD-CLASS TIP

The first requirement of a world-class organization is that its executives and training directors have a keen understanding of global competition.

If you think about your company's strategic positioning first — before all else — and if you have read Perlmutter, Drucker, Prahalad, Hamel, Ghoshal, Doz, Ohmae, Porter, Peters, and Copeland and Griggs, you're in fair shape. To become world-class, executives and training directors must attain a broader and deeper understanding of global competition.

Now that we have described the new global profile, how do you begin developing your managers to fit the profile? One very essential activity that should be encouraged is the habit of reading international periodicals, such as *The Financial Times, Tokyo Business Magazine, The Economist, The Japan Times, Le Point, Business Week, Industry Week, Capital, The Nikkei Weekly, La Monde, We, The International Weekly, World Trade, Fortune, Global Finance, The European Business Journal, Global Executive,* or *Europe* magazine. *The European,* a pan-European newspaper, and CNN reflect the integrated mindset emerging in the global media. Business people interested in staying in tune with changing perspectives should take some time each week to dig into such streams of information. The U.S. Council for International Business in New York, actively involves executives of all sorts in globalization issues. Its committees are an excellent place for executives to get exposure, to learn, and to influence on a global scale. The Global Executive Forum at Georgetown University in Washington, D. C., provides an even more focused setting for discussing global business issues.

Learning to think globally requires a multi-cultural perspective, which is developed by continual exposure to global issues and activities. The process of becoming more globally competitive begins with global information that yields new knowledge, perspectives, and awareness. One does not begin to think globally without a global mental diet. Local and national news programs and publications feed a national mindset; international newspapers and publications feed a global mindset.

Globalized training will not have an optimal impact without this kind of fundamental behavior shift.

Training As a Strategic Change Lever

Too many executives, consultants, and training professionals continue to view training in a narrow and traditional way. Training professionals, in particular, seem to have a tendency to go by the book and design the ultimate course or intervention, regardless of its political relevance to key business strategies. This approach cannot continue. Training must be viewed very differently from how it was viewed just a decade ago. It can no longer be considered an expense or overhead. Rather, training must be categorized as an investment in human capital or simply a cost of doing business.

The world is changing so quickly. Top executives cannot afford to patiently wait four months for a formal needs assessment and job/task analysis to be conducted. Detailed analyses and prescriptive methodologies may only serve to put a competitor that is already behind at a disadvantage. The faster the world moves into the future, the more strategic and intuitive all of us must become to cope effectively.

Training has to lock into a company's strategy. Training processes and management must reflect, and, in some ways, lead the company offensive to become and stay competitive. Training must be the locus through which "nutrients" and continued health enter into the organizational system. Training can help the corporate system accurately "sense" the changes that are occurring or will occur in the outside world and adjust to meet the challenge. Michael Porter, author of *Competitive Advantage of Nations*, has said, "Sustaining and improving competitive position ultimately requires that a firm develop its internal capabilities in areas important to competitive advantage." You need to put world-class training at the center of your strategic thinking.

WORLD-CLASS TIP
World-class training can help the organization "sense" and adjust to changes in the outside world.

Have you ever known an excellent athlete who failed to prepare — train hard — and held a championship position for long? Or, a military team that won a battle without deep concern and attention to preparedness and a strong sense of mission and urgency? The message is simple but hard to implement: **competitions are won by the most highly skilled and the best prepared**. Sun Zu said centuries ago, "The war is won before the battle begins." Today there is really only one type of business competition — global competition, and the field of competitors is broad and mighty in capability. Preparedness becomes the strategic turning point for world-class competition.

World-Class Training Today
Most of the companies people think of as world-class are really just learning the extreme strategic importance of "globalized training," or world-class training. Many companies have numerous training programs that focus on the development of technical skills, basic skills, and traditional input skills. While these are important skills to develop, the key issue in corporations in the twenty-first

century is how to develop global skills and process management skills.

NEC Corporation of Japan offers an example of a company developing a globalized training program. Its president, Tadahiro Sekimoto, explains NEC's process for developing world-class employees:

> It is often said that a business is only as good as its staff, and the same goes for the internationalization or globalization of business. We therefore maintain a large number of personnel programs for internationalization with our international training program at the core. This involves three focal areas:
>
> 1)   Training of international business people,
>
> 2)   Training of personnel for overseas assignments, and
>
> 3)   Training of local managers.
>
> The actual curriculum begins with language courses. English-language training is divided into skill areas such as conversation, writing, and presentation giving. Instruction is also available in Spanish, Portuguese, French, Chinese, and a number of other languages. Next come courses on various aspects of business administration. These include international law, international accounting, international personnel management, international production system, and international marketing as well as... trading procedures, international finance,

and international insurance. [From Jerome M. Rosow's 1989 book, *The Global Marketplace*, pp. 157-158.]

NEC's international training effort also includes international exchanges of personnel. Respect for host cultures is central to their global strategies. NEC sends young workers to NEC Ireland, NEC Electronics (Japan), and elsewhere to help promote mutual understanding. Two-way exchanges take place throughout the NEC worldwide organization.

Unfortunately, few organizations have put together an aggressive training effort that addresses all the issues that are a part of the world-class challenge. This failure is frightening. There is not much time. Amazingly, so many executives, managers, government leaders, and educators still don't get it! The world changes dramatically on a daily basis (technologically, politically, economically, socially); training and related activities **must** change — in focus, purpose, organization, philosophy, and concept. An era of awakening and revitalization is beginning throughout the world, revolutionary in magnitude. No one can escape this revolution. Training must not only keep pace but should be **leading** the revolution.

The university community has begun to focus on the importance of formal education in the global marketplace, too. An advertisement in *Business Week* magazine began, "It's 1990. Do you know where your executives are?" This Columbia University promotion for its executive programs captured the essence of the world-class training concept. The text read:

Whether you head one department or a large corporation, one thing is clear. When you invest in the education of your most promising people, you'll have a distinct advantage over the competition. You'll know where your next generation of leaders will come from. They won't. Give them a plan for lifelong career development — Columbia Executive Programs.

Yes, it's marketing, but Columbia's programs are focused on helping managers to get in synch with current and emerging global business realities. Programs (held in Como, Italy) focus on topics such as international strategy, strategies for 1992, and managing strategic innovation and change.

Other universities have begun developing up-to-date world-class education efforts as well. Among them are programs at Johns Hopkins School of Advanced International Studies, IMD (formerly I.M.E.D.E.), I.N.S.E.A.D., London School of Economics, the University of Maryland's Professional Development Center ("International Competition in the 21st Century"), Penn State's "Global Enterprise" Program, Purdue, Boston University at Brussels ("The Global University"), SDA Bocconi, I.E.S.E., Manchester Business School, the University of Virginia's Darden Graduate School, international programs at Harvard and Stanford, and Georgetown University's Global Executive Program.

A Changing Role For Training Executives

Vision and strategy should constantly drive the training process. In our ever-changing "new world," leaders must be organization changers, trainers must be leaders, and training must be the vehicle for leading, managing, and changing.

And don't forget, leadership begets leadership. Make sure you have your best and boldest leaders in all the right places to facilitate this world-class process, including the leader of your training and development effort. If your training director is not a keen strategist, get somebody new. This whole world-class training operation is too critical to be left to administrative milk-toast types. Get a hard driver, someone with a bold entrepreneurial approach. If you want a world-class organization, there must be a world-class leader in this key slot. You want someone who fits the ultimate global leader profile.

WORLD-CLASS TIP

World-class training is the ultimate vehicle for leading and managing change, for making an organization world-class. Place your training executive at the highest level of your organization, at the side of your chief executive.

Just as corporations must make bolder moves in the marketplace to really "score," training executives must "go for it" to accomplish anything worthwhile in the organization. Thinking big and thinking innovatively about how training can be used to increase the ability of the business to respond to the changing business climate is key to their success. Big changes require big risks and well-planned and well-engineered strategies, and this principle has become as true inside the organization as outside. Training professionals have to equip themselves to be effective in some new roles, such as business analysts, strategists, marketers, planners, statesmen, facilitators, network builders, and sounding boards.

Indeed, the role of training executive deserves to be at the vice-presidential level, considering the broad influence it commands over the organization. Often today, the role is one, two, or even three levels removed from the CEO. That's a strategic error. The most influential leaders in the organization should report directly to the president or CEO so that there is full information flow and optimal influencing of the change process. Training is a key component of the change process — training that provides up-to-date information and the opportunity to develop global thinking skills, common perspectives and purposes, and frameworks in which employees can operate optimally.

≈≈≈

World-class leaders are flexible leaders. They are effective because they listen and influence, through informal rather than formal control and authority. Often they are very bold and entrepreneurial. These characteristics fit well with the needs of the world-class workforce, a workforce of "gold-collar" employees.

Chapter 4

Gold-Collar Employees

4

Gold-Collar Employees

*"He will win whose army is animated by
the same spirit throughout its ranks."*
—Sun Zu, 500 B.C.

Years ago, Robert Kelly wrote about the importance of investing in and developing employees with high skills and effective attitudes—"gold-collar employees." One of the most exciting outcomes of world-class training is that it produces a gold-collar workforce. These employees, as a result of the development and cultivation by their companies, are caring, mission-driven, self-managing, globally-oriented people.   They are **the** engine of enterprise. British businesswoman Jennifer D'Abo has said it well, "I maintain that a business is four walls with people in it."   If an organization is to be competitive, it will be the people who make the difference.

In this chapter, you will learn about the competitive advantage a gold-collar workforce will give you in the global marketplace. You will see that developing world-class employees requires adopting a new perspective about people and that world-class training plays a vital role, because training is the key to the gold-collar workforce.

A New Perspective For Competitive Advantage

As we move into the next century, companies that begin "globalized training" corporate-wide are going to gain a huge advantage — the ultimate competitive advantage — over other global corporations. Some companies keep quiet about this competitive learning process because it has provided them with a significant edge in their markets, and why level the playing field? Other companies feel that training is not their responsibility. The truth depends on how you define education and how much you value competitiveness.

Robert Reich, author of *The Work of Nations*, and Michael Porter, Harvard business professor, believe that the development of the human asset is the most critical single element to global success. Unfortunately, corporate values and policies in many established companies often do not support the individual, innovation, cooperation, or learning. Many company leaders belittle or underestimate their peoples' ability to create a whole new world. That way of thinking simply will not gain companies the competitive edge, especially in the global marketplace.

What is needed today is a new perspective. Traditional attitudes and practices die hard. To change the status quo, corporate leaders must:

- Not merely acknowledge the principle that people are their most important assets, but tout that principle loudly throughout the organization.

- Realize that first and foremost, gold-collar employees are doers, thinkers, creators.

- See that all value, all innovation is a *human* product — a product that does not develop in a vacuum.

- Understand that organizations have to be the soil, water, and nurturer of creative talent.

- Recognize that new business is the direct result of human thinking, effort, and cooperation and that it happens no other way.

- Look pragmatically at what will produce the highest yield for the business investment. When they do that, they will see that the investment in an environment that develops, challenges, and rewards employees really is the key to successful businesses.

Some employees are already gold-collar. They are in total control of their careers, through elaborate personal networks, vision, and strategic thinking. They can literally do whatever they decide to do, because they are connected, perceptive, gutsy individuals who think about all the possibilities and can readily implement them. They demand and consistently earn respect, responsibility, authority, and autonomy. If the organization withholds any of these, it will inevitably lose these world-class employees. The companies that consistently score the big strategic wins think boldly and breed these "can-do" gold-collar employees.

If your organization can have the foresight and ingenuity to retain and challenge the best minds in your industry, you are bound to gain notable advantages over your competition. Process and marketable product are important, but people are the engine that produces value and innovation.

Amazing things can happen in organizations when employees are equipped and empowered and willing to speak their minds. In a 1989 *Industry Week* article, Dalton

Knauss, then chairman and CEO of Square D Company, said:

> There is no formula for becoming global. If you change a basically domestic company into a competitive global force, you should examine every element essential to formulating a successful global strategy. And one of the most vital elements is selecting, involving, and not underestimating the people who are the backbone of your company!

WORLD-CLASS TIP

Basically, there are two types of business organizations: (1) those that treat people as if they are interchangeable or disposable parts and (2) those that treat people as unique, capable learners who are the very engine of the enterprise. If you want your organization to compete successfully in the global marketplace, make sure it falls in the second category.

"Treat employees like partners, and they act like partners," says AT&T CEO Bob Allen. With this principle in mind, he has launched a major campaign to change AT&T's corporate culture, to make it more flexible, responsive, and globally-focused.

The workforce of the next century is not only going to be more diverse and globally-integrated, but also more demanding, more informed, and more highly-skilled. This workforce will test many management teams beyond their current capacity for change and flexibility. But the new perspective requires change for a competitive advantage. Many organizations, such as Xerox, Motorola, Siemens,

British Airways, Hewlett Packard, Honeywell, Corning, Honda, and SAS have been able to achieve an advantage by recognizing that the human capacity to learn and change and add value is central to succeed.

David Kearns, former chairman of Xerox, has stated, "Having a well-educated and empowered workforce is going to change how companies are run." But he added, "We don't even understand what that means yet." One thing it means is that **all** employees will be empowered, and leadership styles will have to change.

Gold Collars For <u>All</u> Employees

Corporations must help all their employees, not just executives and managers, to develop a global perspective and the skills to match.

An industry leader once said, "All workers must manage. All managers must work." This person was predicting the future. This ethic is exactly what is happening inside world-class companies today. Companies are making strategic investments in employee education. Their capabilities are being fully developed to their betterment, to the betterment of the business, and, most importantly, to provide ultimate value to customers. The level of autonomy that is needed by most employees today necessitates higher and broader skills. Knowledge bases and skill sets must be overlapping and broad for organizations to operate effectively in today's changing business climate. Consider the words of Sony Chairman Akio Morita during a 1990 television interview, "In America the corporation is for elite top management. In Japan it is for all employees."

The shift to the team concept reflects a revolutionary change in organizational roles and hierarchy. Flatter (less pyramidal) organizational charts mean that employees will require more training across the board, and in many cases more cross-training. Rosabeth Moss Kanter was quoted in a 1989 *Industry Week* article as saying, "In the 1990s organizations, the team is the competitive advantage." Teams are referred to today as self-managing teams (such as those at General Mills and Southwestern Bell), self-directed workforces, and high-performing teams (like ones at Johnson & Johnson, Xerox, and MCI).

Although involving employees in decision-making processes through teams — Total Employee Involvement (TEI) or Total Quality Management (TQM) — has been a great step forward, it will not be enough in the twenty-first century.

David Kearns comments on employee involvement: "The objective is to ensure that [employees'] talents are applied fully and creatively to problems and opportunities at all levels." Such involvement of all employees at all levels is critical and will be a big change for many companies.

Leaders Who Can Nurture Gold-Collar Employees

A company will have no prospect of developing a gold-collar workforce and directing teams of employees without having world-class leaders. Leaders are the tone-setters for the organization. If they are de-energized, cynical, suspicious, or self-absorbed, the organization has very little chance of nurturing the gold-collar employee.

Think about the key ingredients of a gold-collar organization:

- Clearly-communicated strategic direction

- Core values

- Mission and operating priorities

- Customer focus

- Total quality

- Flexibility

- High performance

A gold-collar environment cannot be mandated or coerced. It can only be nurtured person by person, team by team, so that these key ingredients are fostered and sustained — the job of the world-class leader.

A most pragmatic leader, Donald T. Regan, made an important observation during his time at the helm of Merrill Lynch: "You've got to give loyalty down, if you want loyalty up." The work environment and employees' attitudes are a direct reflection of management's attitudes. As we all know, we reap just what we sow.

Engineering major organizational change not only takes a leader with a sense of urgency, guts, and vision but also insight and patience. It is an extremely complex process involving complex human beings. It is not 100 percent predictable or controllable. Those executives leading major change, including training directors, must be highly intuitive and politically agile. The interpersonal must dominate the mechanical. System and structural changes, to be successful, must follow the building of relationships and understanding. Sometimes change and strategies cannot be affected by just one or a few leaders. The process needs to be supported broadly by training. Training is the key pivotal point for all strategy implementation.

WORLD-CLASS TIP
Employees' attitudes are a direct reflection of management's attitudes.

Investing In And Nurturing Gold-Collar Characteristics

Achieving an environment where gold-collar employees are supported requires an aggressive investment in effective leadership; an open, nurturing environment; and the development of human relationships. Employees who are gold-collar have some very distinguishing characteristics, which include commitment to a vision, commitment to non-stop learning, high motivation without blind loyalty, customer-focus, individualistic behavior, and global-orientation.

Gold-collar employees are committed to a vision. This is a definite hallmark of the world-class workforce. Look at the largest or most successful global enterprises. They have many things in common with their competitors. However, one major difference is the way the employees are committed to their organizations' global vision. And the reason they are committed is because their companies have made a strategic investment in continually upgrading the quality and focus of employee knowledge, perspectives, and skills. And, of course, the way to accomplish that is through training. The only way to create the world-class workforce is to supply world-class training.

Gold-collar employees are committed to nonstop learning. The gold-collar workforce continually hones skills and knowledge to meet rapidly-changing challenges.

People and organizations that desire to remain viable and relevant will institutionalize a fluid, nonstop learning process that will return enormous payoffs. To stay competitive, companies must make learning a top operating priority and a central feature of the corporate culture. As Jerome M. Rosow said in his 1989 book, *The Global Marketplace*, "In today's fierce competitive world, learning something new each day has...become an economic imperative."

A familiar argument in a traditional organization against a large commitment to training goes something like this: "Do you really want us to spend this money on training when we're under such profit pressure?" The response should always be, "Think of training as a strategic investment — the very best kind."

Rigid corporate hierarchies must evaluate the effect gold-collar employees can have on their organization. The differences between employees in traditional and world-class organizations are shown in this comparison:

Employees in a Traditional Organization	**Employees in a World-Class Organization**
Have narrow responsibility and little authority to plan and act.	Are given authority to participate and take action.
Learn on the job or are trained only with skills	Are trained aggressively to have a broad skill-

critically relevant to their current duties — slow, incremental "development."	knowledge base.
Are involved only in large technological or marketing programs.	Capabilities are continually expanded. The company stresses continuous improvement and experimentation.
Work processes remain rigid, even with some meaningful reorganization. No fundamental change in the design and relative importance of work.	Work processes are continually designed to best accomplish strategic objectives.

Some manufacturing and front-line service employees are so heavily conditioned by 10-20 years of oppressive corporate systems and hierarchies, that it may take years for them to unlearn ineffective behavior and absolute mindsets. Leaders must realize this and be understanding role models. They must allow for and invest sufficient management time and energy in continuously examining and improving work processes and in retraining. They are accountable for changing the culture and processes of the organization. There has to be a new comprehensive framework for training and developing employees. John Robinson of Motorola said it well, "Our people are a renewable asset, so we invest in our people, and as we do, their value grows, both to us and to themselves." I agree that training should be useful across the organization, must support corporate strategies and goals, and be treated as a dual investment in people and business.

Remember: Productive, creative, courageous human beings are the ultimate competitive "secret weapon." But employees who embody these qualities are not likely to walk in off the street; you have to develop them. And with today's global marketplace, you have to continue to develop them throughout their careers. "Training is an investment in the future," says Mark Cummings of Case Datatel/Dowty Group plc (a UK-based telecommunications firm).

You can tell that a company is probably serious about people investment as the source of competitive advantage when corporate officers actively participate in training and development activities and the organization is doing one or more of the following:

1. It is allocating 1 percent of total company sales — or more — for ongoing training.

2. It spends $1000 per employee per year for training (as, for example, does L.L. Bean).

3. It ensures that all employees participate in some kind of training each year.

4. It requires a minimum number of hours of training per employee each year (both IBM and Motorola, for example, require 40 hours per employee per year).

But such an investment in training is today the exception rather than the rule.

Gold-collar employees are highly-motivated without blind loyalty. There may no longer be, in the old sense, the "company family" and the deep loyalty that existed in some companies a few decades ago. However, there is still a deep need in the world of business for mutual respect and commitment—indeed, a human partnership. It cannot be consummated by paper and in dollars.

Many people have the mistaken view that if they are loyal to the company, they can expect to be safe and comfortable in their positions. Few things in this world are absolute, and loyalty and trust are, like most things, relative. For most, life is a balance of complex trade-offs between common good and self-interest. Only relative mutual commitment can be achieved between employer and employee. But that is enough if there is ongoing mutual investment.

The motivation of gold-collar employees is to get and provide value through the enterprise they represent. Just making a living is not enough for most employees today. More than ever, people want to make a difference and have significant control over their circumstances and destiny. In today's global marketplace, you don't have to be a CEO to make a difference.

CASE Group plc founder and key leaders spoke often about the employee that makes all the difference in business as "the thinking associate" and the "can-do" employee with a "can-do" attitude. This captures the very essence of the gold-collar employee.

Gold-collar employees are customer-focused. If you want to run a successful business in a competitive environment, you cannot rely on investments alone. You have to be certain your employees are customer-focused. Forget about who is doing what for a moment and just consider what your organization could be like if old barriers and mindsets were thrown aside in favor of total concentration on the customers' needs.

Jan Carlson, chief executive of Scandinavian Airlines (SAS), has some bold ideas about global competitiveness. His motto is, "Make decisions so that the customer's needs are satisfied immediately." He says, "SAS treats people as individuals, not as a collective. This applies to both customers and employees." Carlson also notes, "In order to satisfy customer requirements, people have to be trained to take responsibility and to create their own authority."

Japanese companies do not stand still but are continuously driving to serve customers around the world with goods and services of the highest possible quality. This drive for perfection in producing products and services of the highest value reflects a tremendous will on the part of employees to win in the global marketplace. Japanese companies are clearly moving targets. This kind of aggressive, relentless push toward superior performance is virtually unmatchable.

An important element in being customer-focused is to conduct market research to determine customer requirements. For example, Italtel's R&D commitment to market research is reflected by the level of investment in this field, which reached 152 billion lire in 1986, equivalent to 11.5 percent of sales. This percentage is in line with that of the most innovative American and Japanese companies.

Another way companies focus on customers is by delivering high quality. Indeed, many leading companies have concentrated much of their attention and resources on

TQM (total quality management). High quality is one of the strategic imperatives today that can only be attained though effective, ongoing world-class training. Creatively and effectively providing value to customers globally must be the top operating priority. Political maneuvering cannot be allowed to derail this world-class philosophy. It must be primary for companies to achieve sustainable success in the global marketplace.

Gold-collar employees are individualistic. The gold-collar workforce is an individualistic rather than a conforming workforce. Multiple motivations and diverse values must be encouraged and managed effectively throughout the organization. Managers cannot assume that employees are driven by the same philosophies. Some gold-collar employees are upwardly mobile, some seek groups, and some seek interesting work. Development tracks should be tailored for each one. The new workforce will require strategic career counseling for each employee as part of the nurturing that gold-collar employees require.

Executives spend incredible amounts of time, energy, and money chasing after the ultimate competitive advantage, and it is right under their noses—people! What people are capable of doing and creating when they are properly equipped and valued is absolutely incredible. Although people are often challenged, they are seldom equipped or valued at a high enough level. Consider the oppressive "need-to-know" mentality that still lingers in many traditional organizations. **In the world-class organization, everyone needs to know,** and very little is really proprietary or confidential among committed and mission-minded teams of professionals. All employees, top to bottom, should be equipped with a keen sense of the ethical, the innovative, the global. There is a continual sense of both urgency and preparedness. Today's global marketplace warrants both.

Gold-collar employees are globally-oriented. Do you currently have a gold-collar workforce that is fully equipped to compete with the very best workers around the world? If not, how can you go about remedying this global skills discrepancy? The key is to get employees attuned to differences and change. People in different parts of the world conduct business differently, and things are changing rapidly everywhere.

Barry J. New, vice president of Rolls Royce, Inc., says regarding U.S.-British differences, "It is important to try not to fall into the trap of believing that even though we speak more or less the same language, we approach problems and issues from the same perspective." Forty percent of U.S. exports already go to Europe. It is familiar territory to many. This familiarity is deceiving in many ways, because there are great cultural differences. Leaders who fail to take such differences into account and prepare accordingly may now find themselves at a major competitive disadvantage when they try to do business with Europeans.

To summarize, any organization that cultivates employees who are thinkers, creators, and doers, and that knows the power of teamwork and sheer will, is developing a gold-collar workforce that can be expected to deliver significant results. Although many companies have not discovered the value of creating a gold-collar workforce, some have, and they are seeing a high level of commitment and extraordinary results. More and more leaders seem to be seeing the strategic need for this kind of investment in their employees.

WORLD-CLASS TIP
The best strategic investment any enterprise can make is one that continually upgrades the quality and focus of employee knowledge, perspectives, and skills.

Developing Gold-Collar Workers Demands Focus

World-class training is not magic. It takes hard work, fast thinking, tremendous skill, competitive awareness, and a directed customer focus to implement and manage. Today, the areas on which a company might focus world-class training include:

- The customer

- Team process and team learning

- Competitive thinking

- Innovation

- Total quality and continuous improvement

- Change management

- Problem-solving techniques

- Effective leadership in a global context

- Technology management

- Telecomputing skills

- Cross-cultural and language skills

Setting out in a new direction can be difficult, but some firms are already cutting the path.

Examples Of Gold-Collar Workforces

Some of the organizations that develop gold-collar workforces are: Physio-Control, Apple Computer, Analog Devices, Johnson & Johnson, Fiat, Motorola, Honda, Sherwin-Williams, CASE, Federal Express, and Marriott. Many of the same big names keep coming up, but there are some smaller firms as well.

Honda offers an example of a company's success as a result of commitment to its employees. With estimated revenues of $24 billion and 66 plants, Honda operates in 35 countries in Asia, Europe, Latin America, and North America (including nearly 8,000 "associates" in Ohio producing nearly 75 percent of its Accord model). Honda enjoys a reputation for technological superiority and customer service excellence, providing high value at reasonable costs. Consultant Larry Miller refers to Honda as "something new: a world-embracing company with a world-embracing philosophy" (which may be close to the heart of the concept of a world-class corporation).

Soichiro Honda began the road to long-term global competitiveness by asking the question, "How can we motivate our production people to feel the same way about their jobs as our managers do?" People involvement at Honda is key. Indeed, many observers and associates attribute much of Honda's success to its excellent use of its human resources. Honda doesn't just *treat* their associates well, they *equip* their associates *fully* to meet the world-class challenge.

John Christianson, former manager of associate development at Honda/HAM, once explained to me, "We want associates to use their heads as well as their hands. When a company uses only its employees' hands, it's merely buying them. But when the company solicits employees' thoughts, their hearts are eventually won because the employees have a total commitment to their company."

A world leader in providing customer satisfaction, Marriott has taken the bold move of treating employees like customers and has actively engaged them in the business of engineering a positive experience for all Marriott customers. The focus of these efforts is to stay in synch with customer expectations. According to customer research, checking in and getting settled well are key to the customer's overall experience with the hotel. "If interactions with the customer are well-orchestrated by courteous, well-trained staff, the customer is likely to enjoy a positive perception and experience of Mariott," notes William Tieffel, president of the company's international hotel and resorts division.

By engaging hotel associates in this way and providing excellent training and feedback loops, Marriott is able to keep its "friendly" and "superefficiency" indexes high. This pays off in repeat business and motivated staff. It's a winning combination, and Marriott is capturing the essence of "gold collar employees" worldwide. People who are engaged, focused, and continually learning are the engine of long-term business success. Marriott is a most visible and striking example of how a "well invested in" workforce can make all the difference in the global marketplace.

Fiat, Italy's largest private company, is another example of an organization that has invested heavily in its employees. It has concentrated great effort on innovation and management development, and it is seeing the results. It has created organizational and management systems, expanded training centers, developed a common culture, and established a modern and loyal professional workforce that is multinational. Fiat is determined to continue improving its already streamlined organization and to pay a substantial amount of attention to the development of human resources.

In another example, change has been brought about at CASE Group plc. Mark Cummings, vice president of manufacturing, states simple operating goals: improve quality, enhance customer delivery, and improve gross margins. To meet these goals, he focuses much of his attention on the people side of the business. After spending several years designing the ultimate manufacturing process, he comments, "Automation can only take you so far." Cummings is enthusiastic about Case Group's competitive prospects. High responsiveness, team problem solving, innovative thinking by employees, and high quality are all the basis for this new energy and focus. These days, Case Group is consistently hearing good things from customers. Cummings and his well-knit team are determined to provide world-class products and service.

Sherwin Williams' Specialty Products Group and Dutch Boy Operations provide good examples of how a company was able to use world-class training as a powerful tool in the transformation of the organization. During the early

1980s, Sherwin-Williams was in turnaround mode with Jack Breen at the helm. Tough circumstances during those tight times forced the company to be both innovative and resourceful. Attempting to move from an old-line low-tech position to an aggressive medium-tech position, the organization faced increasing foreign competition in the sundries division and intensified competition from the regional producers in the paint division. A first step was to reorient and re-equip a seasoned, stable workforce — the traditional "model" workforce.

The company's specialty products operation in Deshler, Ohio had a highly competent workforce, but its remoteness meant that awareness of global competition needed to be increased. The situation called for people development and continuous improvement in processes and technology. Dieter Kulicke — German-born and raised in Canada and the U.S., with a very interesting vantage point on international business, was then director of manufacturing. The company focused its attention on human resource development and critical capital investment. After several years of investing this way, both quality and profit margins had increased by a factor of three. Making what is good even better — that's part of what global competitiveness is all about.

At Sherwin-Williams' Richmond, Kentucky plant and in the Consumer Division's union-free sites, the company was an early pioneer of pay-for-knowledge-and-skills systems, the team concept, performance management, and continuous employee improvement and learning. Retraining existing employees in new ways of thinking paid great dividends.

Deshler, Richmond, and Dutch Boy Operations plants are still model, high-performing organizations in the paint industry. Kulicke's counterpart with Dutch Boy, Jim Kearney, is quick to emphasize the world-class organization's need to constantly retrain and to develop new skills, positive attitudes, and broader knowledge base.

Retaining Employees With World-Class Training

In addition to retraining people to be and produce the best, world-class training can help an organization retain the best people. Most Fortune 500 top executives don't realize just how stifling and oppressive their controlled hierarchies have become to their employees. Business is no fun for anyone, including the customer! Employee motivation and initiative are squelched. The best employees continually move up and out at a tremendous hidden cost to corporations. Employees who stay often lose their enthusiasm and become corporate conformists. This type of retention is not in the best interest of company stakeholders. This cycle has to be broken completely in this decade, and a new corporate culture and breed of employee must be born.

WORLD-CLASS TIP

One of the most attractive features of world-class training is its positive effect on employee retention. It can lead to an upward spiral of employee retention and development. World-class training fosters retention because it develops and challenges people, and retention allows greater individual development because proportionately fewer resources need to be invested in newcomer orientation.

To retain the best employees, companies will have to compete for them by providing the most empowering and enjoyable work environment possible. Many companies have undertaken what I call industry shift retraining; however, retraining simply does not offer the potential benefits that developing and keeping the best can.

The Gold-Collar Challenge

A quiet revolution is happening in many corporations today. Employees, at many levels and across many disciplines, are already well-educated, highly-skilled, well-informed, and empowered. As soon as they are given opportunities and are fully-equipped, they will be ready for any competitive challenge. The *Wall Street Journal* quoted James Perkins, senior vice president of personnel for Federal Express, as saying that there "is tremendous pressure because of competitiveness to continue to improve quality and productivity and lower cost to the customer." There is a tremendous challenge before today's global workforce to demonstrate quick thinking, fast acting, and global understanding. However, the greatest challenge of all, is to help corporate leaders find ways of fully engaging a demanding, diverse, and globablized workforce. Winning in the global marketplace certainly is a "gold-collar" prospect.

Perkins continues, "I think there is an increasing awareness that a company's human resources are a competitive weapon. There is an awareness that well-trained, highly-motivated employees really can make a difference in terms of improved productivity, improved quality."

In this decade, companies everywhere have the opportunity to change how they operate; how they serve and produce; and how they are perceived by customers, employees, and analysts.

≈≈≈

For all the money spent on traditional training by multinational firms in the last decade, the world of business could have been totally revamped using world-class training. With world-class training, employees will learn a new and vital way of thinking about the world and all the business opportunities continually spawned by change. These employees will have a deep conviction that they, as a unified, gold-collar workforce, can shape the very future of the world. With world-class training, new companies can exist with new corporate cultures, new services, new products, new projects, new market share, and new hope.

Chapter 5

The Cross-Cultural Maze

5

The Cross-Cultural Maze

*"Today we operate in a world market that demands
a more culturally sensitive management....Savvy
organizations are getting the message about the
multiple values of cross-cultural training."*
—Philip Harris and Robert Moran
Managing Cultural Differences, 1987

The world is filled with people of diverse cultures and very different perceptions, expectations, and motivations. Knowing how to think and behave effectively in these different cultures is not easy. In fact, it is complicated and confusing— like trying to find the way out of a maze. Edward T. Hall, pioneer of the cross-cultural field, says that an understanding of different cultures may well be "the most important asset in meeting the challenge of our times."

This chapter provides:

- Illustrations of cross-cultural situations in the world marketplace

- A description of challenges to organizations that do not prepare their employees with cross-cultural skills

93

- Examples of cross-cultural "disconnect"

- A discussion of cross-cultural training as a prerequisite for success in the global marketplace

- Examples of companies that have implemented cross-cultural training

- A description of culturally appropriate training

The Multicultural Marketplace

Picture a California-manufactured airbus powered by British engines, while a competing airbus flies on Canadian wing assemblies. Envision a Frenchman appointed as president of the U.S.-domiciled IBM World Trade Corporation, while an American establishes a Swiss-based international mutual fund. These situations provide a snapshot of the cross-cultural maze of the marketplace today. Other examples that illustrate this maze are:

- ICI and Einmont's joint venture, European Vinyls Corporation, have acquired two Italian plastics manufacturers.

- The Germans are getting into the mail order business in the former USSR.

- The British are teaming up with a Russian partner and building "Pizza Huts" in the C. I. S.

- They're drinking Pepsi and eating at McDonalds in Moscow and will soon have their own Levi Strauss jeans factory.

- Ford, Coca Cola, GE, and Procter & Gamble have gone into major manufacturing ventures in Eastern Europe.

- DMS, the Dutch chemical group, and Rubbermaid (U.S.) have set up a joint manufacturing and marketing effort in Europe.

- The Saudis have purchased Texaco's oil refineries and marketing division.

- Grand Met now owns the Pillsbury doughboy.

- Bell Atlantic is investing $3 billion in the EC (European Community) countries in joint ventures with national telecommunications administrations and acquisitions of local companies in specialized fields. Bell opened its European headquarters in Brussels to work closely with its main suppliers: AT&T, Siemens, Northern Telecom, and Alcatel.

- Toyota has displaced Chrysler in the race of the "Top Three in U.S. Auto Sales."

- Apple Computer has initiated a strategy to simultaneously penetrate Europe and select Pacific Rim markets.

- Selective Software, in Santa Cruz, California, has developed PC software that automatically translates letters into Spanish, Italian, German, or French.

- IBM and Computerland have set up shop in that financial powerhouse of a kingdom, Luxemburg.

- According to *Europe* magazine, last year Compaq Computer's EC sales alone were $1 billion.

- Foreign investment in the U.S. has surpassed the $2 trillion mark.

More and more organizations are becoming culturally diverse. Management teams are becoming multicultural. We can expect that this will be the norm in the twenty-first century. U.S. firms will not always have Americans at the helm, British firms will not always have British nationals as chief executives, and even Japanese firms will increasingly use local national managers to operate local operations. Because these teams will consist of people with diverse and strong viewpoints, consensus will not be easy to attain. Active negotiation will be required on a regular basis. "Group think" will be quite impossible, and autocratic or totalitarian chief executives will not survive.

Winning yesterday has very little to do with winning today or tomorrow. There's no going back, just forward —

out into the global marketplace—and briskly. Companies today are moving too slowly into the new global business reality. Talking about yesterday's strategies in today's jargon is "an old news story" any way you package it.

The Need For Intercultural Skills

According to Dr. Robert Moran, one of the most underdeveloped sets of skills in managers across the globe is intercultural skills. The lack of these skills can — and many times does — cause global firms to fail.

Much of the lack of understanding of other cultures is a result of our attitudes. Sixty-seven percent of HR executives surveyed in the 1990 *HR Executive* magazine indicated that "international acclimation" was not going to be an important item in coming years. This attitude is just unfathomable! How out of touch can we be?

Consider that American business people can visit Asia once and become "knowledgeable," visit twice and are "expert" — all with a narrow set of expectations and without knowing the language. Americans somehow can live in another part of the world for years and still not learn enough about the culture and local mindset to add real value to the local business process and customers. The sad fact is that executives and managers without proper cross-cultural preparation can have the same "international experience" over and over, with a focus on business tasks that somehow precludes a deeper understanding of cultures.

American managers in particular seem to have some liabilities in the area of cross-cultural effectiveness. Even those who have had cross-cultural training sometimes fail at building the right kind of social bridges in business. Jerry Underwood, a former director for the U.S. Department of Commerce, says, "Americans have a natural inward business philosophy that leads to ethnocentric behavior...." Notwithstanding the fact that *American Demographics* magazine surveys show 71 percent of Americans have visited a foreign country, Americans still tend to have a seriously imbalanced view of the world.

Most international managers don't perceive themselves as ethnocentric at all. Because they are world jet-setters, they feel they completely understand the foreign manager's point of view. However, they seldom do. Their perception that they do is largely just a matter of self-deception and ignorance. Learning different languages and the meaning of cultures is not something automatic that can be absorbed through multiple exposures. In the words of one executive, Americans in particular are "still deficient in their international comparative thinking." And all this talk of "global thinking" is essentially worthless unless it translates into culturally enlightened *behavior*.

What is your global IQ? Do you know:

- How many countries belong to the U.N.?

- What the EFTA is?

- What ASEAN, OAU, and OECD stand for?

- How the Ex-Im Bank works?

- How to speak Russian, Hungarian, Swahili, Korean, or Japanese?

- How stock markets work in Tokyo, London, Paris, Frankfurt, and Sydney?

- How Korean consumers think?

- What the latest issue of *The European, The Economist, The European Journal of International Affairs, Business Tokyo Magazine* or *The Japan Times* say about what is happening in your industry around the globe?

- What a "Kangaroo Group" is?

- What areas of business are addressed in the EC's 23 DG's?

The problem of ethnocentricity is not limited to Americans. Whether your company is a British, Japanese, or French firm operating in the United States or an American or Korean firm operating in Spain, there will be cultural nuances that cannot be fully conveyed even by local nationals. Particularly, there are details about foreign markets that cannot be fully appreciated by nonlocals unless they have intensive training about and prolonged exposure to those markets.

Whether you are a manager at NCR's Dundee, Scotland, operation, a technician at the Suburu-Izuzu plant in Lafayette, Indiana in the United States, or an international marketing executive located in Geneva, Switzerland, many of the same issues are relevant. In general, every time people transact business across cultural lines, something happens

— something gets lost. Somehow, full meaning does not get transferred, and communication, relationships, and business results often suffer.

Consider the insight provided by a simple statement made by a manager of an international trading company: "In Germany, your product is most important to your success; in Japan, it is the human relationships you build. Without them you will not succeed." There are some business people today operating unsuccessfully with German and Japanese businesses because even this basic knowledge has not penetrated their thinking yet.

Any American manager seeking to be a world-class leader can gain insight from the following list of the most common stereotypes of Americans held by foreigners. This "ugly American" list reveals in some sense a greater reality, because it shows how others see us. Of course, a list could be compiled for the stereotypic views of any nationality as seen by foreigners.

Stereotypes of Americans

- Outgoing, friendly

- Informal (not necessarily positive)

- Loud, rude, boastful, immature

- Hard-working (maybe too much so)

- Extravagant, wasteful

- Think they have all the answers

- Not class-conscious

- Disrespectful of authority

- Racially prejudiced

- Know little about other countries

- All American women: promiscuous

- All wealthy

- Generous

- Always in a hurry

   (Source: L. Robert Kohls, *Survival Kit for Overseas Living*, 1984)

The Cross-Cultural Disconnect

Let's consider anecdotal examples of cross-cultural "disconnects" (which are situations that occur when cultural differences are not thoroughly understood). A personal experience shared with me by Peter Danos, a retired international operating executive for 3M in Europe, will give you an idea of the kind of situation that requires a manager to have more than a superficial understanding of the cultural motivations of his employees. Danos was the director of a manufacturing facility in Spain and was having some difficulty establishing the starting time for his staff meeting. His managers seemed unable to get to his important operations and scheduling meetings on time.

Knowing the culture, he tried to think of some way he could improve punctuality without shaming or hurting the professional pride of his managers. Reminders, prodding, and persuading had not yielded the desired results. So, he did what any other fast-thinking global manager would do—he entered into a contest agreement with his managers. The agreement was that each week he would give a special award to the manager who was late to meetings more often than other managers.

The first week of the contest came and went, and Danos had his secretary bring in a silver tray to present to the "winner." On the tray was a rather funny-looking cactus plant. As he presented the special award, he reminded the winner and others that, as agreed upon, the award had to be exhibited on the desk of the recipient for an entire week. The winner reluctantly took the cactus on the silver platter and carried it back to his office with glass windows all around. As employees passed by, they chuckled to themselves at the odd sight.

The word spread. Within a week, Danos' tardiness problem had been creatively and effectively solved. The other managers did not want that silly thing on their desks! Being on time was a small price to pay to avoid the effects of this shrewd ploy. In that particular context, it was the effective action to take. In other places, perhaps other solutions would have been more suitable.

To highlight the significance of cultural differences in business, Nancy Adler tells the following:

When a Danish manager works with a Saudi and the Saudi states that the plant will be completed on time, "Insha'a Allah" ("If God is willing"), the Dane rarely believes that God's will is really going to influence the construction progress. He continues to see the world from his parochial Danish perspective and assumes that "En shah allah" is just an excuse for not getting the work done, or is meaningless altogether. Similarly, when Balinese workers' families refuse to use birth control methods, explaining that it will break the cycle of reincarnation, few Western managers really consider that there is a possibility that they will be reborn a number of times. Instead, they assume that the Balinese do not understand or are afraid of Western medicine. [*International Dimensions of Organizational Behavior*, pp. 66-67, 1986]

Adler suggests some role-reversal exercises to develop sympathy and reduce parochialism. They will force you to "see the other person as he or she really is, and not as a mere reflection of yourself."

As director of corporate training with CASE Group plc, a British telecommunications firm, I had an enlightening experience when I first trained British managers in performance management. While growing up, I had lived abroad and had known many people from the U.K. over the years. Nevertheless, certain cultural subtleties had not really registered. During my presentation of the performance management model, it became clear that some of the primary assumptions of the model were not part of the managers' experience or value base. Performance management seemed much too control-oriented to them. They found it preposterous to think that managers, regardless of their management status, could "engineer" others' performance. As a result of their culture, they had a very different view of how influence could and should be used to accomplish business outcomes.

A couple of hours into the first session, I knew I was going to have to alter my approach, so I solicited input from the group and tried to key in on the information they provided. Their input became the basis for adapting the model; the approach had to be softened and made more pragmatic to accommodate the participants' frames of reference. After we finished, many participants stayed to further discuss the implications of this approach in particular situations they were then facing. There was value in the performance management process, but my approach and perspective had to be altered to be effective. It took moving beyond fundamental cultural differences.

Many of the cultural differences that need to be understood by managers and professionals in global corporations are so fundamental that the mind can barely perceive the need for understanding. Take, for instance, the differences in management philosophy and business models from country to country. Although culturally sensitive, many U.S. executives still assume that their business approach is the best because it is theirs. They must learn to explore and blend business models and management philosophies as appropriate in each cultural context in which they operate.

Internationally respected interculturist, Pierre Casse of I.M.E.D.E. in Lausanne, Switzerland, says, "The more we talk about globalization, the more we must learn to cope with and manage cultural differences."

Cross-Cultural Training Prerequisite For Success

The complexity of cross-cultural transactions that involve employees at various corporate levels is both staggering and confusing, and yet there still doesn't seem to be a sense of urgency for training and developing all employees, especially among the executive elite of certain corporate cultures. Many executives and training professionals still see cross-cultural and international training as something reserved for the "top," or for international marketing personnel, and definitely as something separate from other training. This notion is simply no longer appropriate. If the acceleration of globalization causes anything, it should cause a greater awareness of the need for cross-cultural understanding at all levels of an organization, as more and more business is conducted in the global marketplace.

If you fail to properly equip and inform your first-line, mid-level, or behind-the-scenes employees, you are only adding to your own competitive disadvantage. Be smart. Trust your people. Invest in them with energy, confidence, and foresight, and you will be on the road to winning in the global marketplace.

The development and mastery of cross-cultural skills, a knowledge of international business, and training in foreign languages at all levels are prerequisites for companies to become and remain world-class. Companies will not develop the necessary competitive edge without system-wide training in these areas. Administrative, support, and technical personnel *cannot* be left out of this learning process, which is critical to global competitiveness. No one can expect employees to perform in a world-class fashion if they haven't been fully equipped to deal with the world-class challenge.

After having talked with more than one hundred training executives worldwide, I have come to the conclusion that relatively few organizations engage in cross-cultural and foreign language training. Rather than thinking about whether corporations should be providing this training, we should be determining the advantages corporations can gain through cross-cultural understanding and language capability.

I was amazed to see in the 1989 *Training Magazine* industry survey that there was not even a category called cross-cultural skills, and only 12 percent of companies responding said they were conducting any foreign language training. I am not sure how companies can be serious about becoming globally competitive when they are investing so little to globally equip their employees. Even reputable global corporations that spend millions of dollars on training in the latest manufacturing methods and management development techniques will not be able to maintain their world-class status if this global, cross-cultural piece is missing from their training.

And the problem extends beyond corporate training. Patrick Morgan, manager of personnel at Bechtel Civil, Inc., predicts that human resource professionals are going to be required to learn to handle a variety of global and cross-cultural issues. Believing that the cross-cultural component is missing from many management development programs, he says, "International HR training needs more work. Different HR textbooks are indicative of the course context of typical HR degree programs. We have a long way to go in globalizing our approach."

Peter Danos sees the cross-cultural issue as central to the effective management of the global corporation. According to Danos, there are a number of key issues that managers and professionals need to be sensitive to in the cross-cultural arena. He encourages the development of an empathy for second, third, fourth, and fifth cultures. Business practices; traditions and norms; legal differences; the view of family, work, government, and religion; personal privacy; education; labor relations; and social customs — all deserve special study and attention. Executives and managers operating across cultures should avoid major liability by learning all they can learn about these topics, well before they get involved with the markets they represent.

Craig Storti, author of *The Art of Crossing Cultures* (1989), has a unique way of helping executives and professionals get keen personal insight into many cultures, starting with their own. He uses excerpts from well-known literature and popular films to fully convey differences between cultures.

Eric Novotny, vice president of international marketing for COMSAT Systems Division, shares an important insight about doing business in various cultures. He says it is important to think in terms of "playing by their rules on their turf and to be **aware** of them at all times." With globalization at full tilt, I might go one step further and say that learning multiple sets of cultural rules and playing by them adeptly will give incredible strategic advantage to firms.

The foremost expert on cross-cultural issues, Edward T. Hall, shares some interesting insights into doing business with the Japanese in his 1987 book, *Hidden Differences* (pp.146-147). Some of these differences may be almost impossible for some executives to adjust to, but if they really intend to compete seriously, they must learn to adjust.

1. Be patient—very, very patient. Don't push; allow plenty of time for "nemawahsi" (laying the groundwork). Be ready to jump through hoops "of trust and acceptance."

2. Take the long view. The Japanese are not interested in the short-term relationship.

3. Don't come to teach. Come to learn.

4. Learn the language!

5. Learn new ways to communicate.

6. Respect consensus and compromise.

7. Accept personal responsibility for your job.

8. Be thoroughly prepared.

9. Learn to depend on your Japanese advisors. You will need coaching every step of the way.

10. Pay great attention to detail.

Did you notice how many times the word *learn* was used? This choice is not accidental. To be effective globally, you must be in a learning mode, and it requires training. Hall also suggests that you select and train your very best people for Japan, and plan on them staying for more than just a few years. He emphasizes that cultural and language training should be mandatory.

One of the most strategically valuable cross-cultural skills is international negotiating. In *Multicultural Manager*, Pierre Casse highlights five competencies related to this high-payback skill:

- To be able to practice empathy and see the world as others see it.

- To be able to demonstrate the advantages of what one's proposals offer, so that the counterparts in the negotiation will be willing to change.

- To be able to manage stress and cope with ambiguous situations as well as unpredictable demands.

- To be able to express one's own ideas in such a way that the people one negotiates with will objectively and fully understand what one has in mind.

- To be sensitive to the cultural background of others and adjust suggestions one wants to make to the existing constraints and limitations.

Casse talks about learning about cross-cultural issues on three levels: (1) within multicultural work teams, (2) between teams, and (3) between organizations in the marketplace (alliances and customers). He feels the same urgency I do to invest in cross-cultural training and is moving roughly in the same direction with his consulting, training, and teaching efforts. You can read more of Pierre Casse's view in his books *Training for the Multicutural Manager* (1982) and *Training for the Cross-Cultural Mind* (1981).

Clearly, European and Japanese multinational corporations see increasingly high value in cross-cultural and foreign language training. In Europe, the Center for International Briefing in the U.K. and Berlitz are well-used resources for this type of training. Some say European and Japanese firms are willing to invest in this way because of their long-term orientation and global business strategies. This phenomenon needs to be studied closely, because there is no doubt that these companies discern a clear strategic advantage by investing in employees in this way.

The intercultural experts cited encourage investment in cross-cultural training. I suggest this investment should be ongoing and multilevel. To get an ample supply of "global profiles"—employees with the skills needed for the global marketplace—corporations must revamp their training and development efforts.

WORLD-CLASS TIP

Cross-cultural and language skills are prerequisities to becoming and remaining world-class. Companies will not develop the necessary competitive edge without system-wide training in these areas.

Multicultural Training—Not Just For Expatriates

For many years, only the large multinational corporations conducted any international training, and even then, it was usually limited to employees being assigned overseas. There was nothing wrong with this approach in the 1960s, but today global training is clearly for *everyone*.

Unfortunately, to date most of what has been written on cross-cultural and language training is aimed at international assignees only. Correspondingly, much of the "international training" that is conducted is focused on the international assignee. Of course, employees going abroad do need special cross-cultural and foreign language training, but they probably need more than they are getting. Untrained expatriates roaming the world should be seen as the potential corporate liabilities they are. Their training shouldn't be left to on-the-job training!

Training expatriates is just one dimension of the training corporations need to do to remain competitive in the global arena. The American Management Association (AMA) and many companies are still taking a 1960s and1970s approach to international training issues, focusing on international assignees only. What about the people back home who interface, design, manufacture for, or support people in globalized markets?

WORLD-CLASS TIP

No matter where employees work in the organization, they need to understand global competition and have global perspectives and competencies.

One person who has articulated the need to develop cross-cultural awareness in all employees is Lewis Griggs, author of *Going International*. Griggs says cross-cultural training is "absolutely essential" and that "anyone doing business needs to be attuned to cross-cultural issues in the global arena. There is," he continues, "general cross-cultural training needed for overseas assignments...even for those staying home." He advises that companies should "learn before making a costly mistake." This view is echoed by Black & Decker top executive Mike Convey, president of Price-Pfister, Inc. He says that "American management lacks a real sensitivity to cultural differences" in the global marketplace.

Examples Of World-Class Cross-Cultural Training

Just what kind of cross-cultural training does an integrated world-class training approach provide? Let me share some examples with you.

INTELSAT has employees representing more than one hundred countries. Chris Brown, former manager of training and development, explains that in the management development program, one day is allotted totally to "Managing in a Multicultural Environment." A more intensive program called "Working Internationally: Skills, Competence, and Performance" focuses managers on differences in cultural assumptions and styles and develops greater awareness and understanding. Language offerings include multiple levels of French and Spanish.

COMSAT has conducted extensive cross-cultural skills training, foreign language training, and international round tables and briefings that are open to **all** employees. Some 30 plus "global" training courses are offered. These include Global Marketing, Global Telecommunications, International Negotiating, Cross-Cultural Shortcourse, Import/Export, Europe 1992, Eastern Europe Update, Glasnost and the USSR, Japan and the Pacific Rim. Foreign languages offered include Russian, Japanese, Spanish,

French, and German. Business French, Business Spanish, Business German, and Business Japanese focus on telecommunications and commercial vocabulary in each language.

Philip Gordon, Ph.D. at Johns Hopkins SAIS, among others, has put together "up-to-the-minute" briefings on Europe, Eastern Europe, the C. I. S., and Japan to serve as course materials in COMSAT's international series. The series is an integral part of the world-class training approach. There is heavy emphasis on getting new perspectives on changing globalized markets and on the cross-cultural skills necessary to operate effectively in them.

Culturally Appropriate Training

As my example of training British managers in performance management showed, an important part of "globalized training" is the whole issue of culturally appropriate materials, training, processes, and philosophy. Many large American companies, and some Japanese companies, have for so long assumed that the best way to train is "their way." Regardless of whether the employee (or manager) was in Singapore, Hong Kong, or Los Angeles, one basic style of training was supposed to work. Non-national instructors were often sent to teach "the corporate way." I am not suggesting that companies shouldn't try to reinforce corporate mission and values through training, only that the context, content, delivery, and methodology must all reflect that of the learner to optimize learning.

The training director of a major international ocean freight (shipping) company explained to me that his company is moving quickly toward a globalized training process, with thousands of employees around the globe linked by information technology. The need for culturally appropriate training that is consistent throughout the organization has become a critical issue. Many firms keep expatriates in several key posts in every country in which they operate, but all employees must be properly trained to be effective — and it has to make sense to *them.*

So, what you have to figure out is what is important to trainees in various countries. Fortunately, most people who work for a company based in another country seem to place a high value on training. Some years ago, *Harvard Business Review* ran an article entitled, "Understand Your Overseas Workforce." In a survey of salesmen, technical personnel, and service personnel, 16 out of 25 countries ranked *training* among the top four most important goals — before challenge, autonomy, earnings, or advancement.

For companies conducting training around the globe, Lennie Copeland of Copeland and Griggs, suggests eight rules for conducting training in local situations [*Going International*, 1989]:

1. Make training meaningful from the perspective of the trainee.

2. Training groups should consist of people with similar backgrounds destined for similar jobs.

3. Conscientiously try to gain respect and trust.

4. Accommodate training to second- or third-language discomfort.

5. Adjust to learning habits.

6. Yield to "differences in thinking" problems.

7. Revamp training schedules to local cultural norms.

8. Be venturesome and courteous.

We must move beyond cultural differences. Unfortunately, cross-cultural disconnects happen every day. Training that is not adapted to local cultures, for various reasons, fails to achieve all it could if it were properly designed and planned. Many international HRD executives and educators tell real horror stories. But the outlook is bright. Learning more about the important differences in frames of reference used by counterparts, partners, or customers of other cultures could be one of the best investments you ever make. There is so much of value to learn that corporations need to become extremely aggressive in how they go about equipping employees around the world to work in the global marketplace. The key is to design training programs that are culturally appropriate.

WORLD-CLASS TIP
Corporations must become extremely aggressive in preparing employees around the world to work in the global marketplace—and to do this with culturally appropriate training programs.

≈≈≈

By definition, to lead means to have bold ideas and to take bold action. World-class leadership requires a bold and innovative ongoing investment in people. To develop the global corporation, you must develop managers and professionals who are comfortable in multiple cultures and proficient in the languages of those cultures. This objective is a most essential part of world-class training.

Chapter 6

Big Picture Training

6

Big Picture Training

"You are paying your key people to see the big picture."
—*Harvey Mackay*
Author and Consultant

When top management encounters employee resistance to change and improvement, the executives often ask, "Don't they understand the big picture?" The reality is that employees do not ordinarily understand the big picture because it has not usually been shared with them in any regular or meaningful way. Employees at all levels need a shared way of thinking about change. This process should be a fluid, flexible one that allows for a playful, creative, resourceful approach to effect changes. I call this process "Big Picture Training." For world-class training to be effective, Big Picture Training must be included as one of the key elements. World-class companies realize that informing people and providing a system in which people connect with one another across the organization are keys to constant revitalization.

The big picture is not just for "key people" unless those key people include workers at every level of the organization. Indeed, business success over the next twenty years hinges on how well businesses involve their workers. Globalization is steadily forcing companies to engage and equip employees more aggressively and continually. Most managers know deep down that only involved, informed, respected, supported people are committed to the enterprise. The question is how to make this happen and keep it going.

At Sherwin-Williams, we started Big Picture Training with some fine people at the plant in rural Deshler, Ohio that I discussed earlier. After several discussions with my boss, Dieter Kulicke, director of manufacturing, we decided to get working groups together to talk about the competitiveness of the business. We were under siege from foreign and small regional competitors. Deshler employees, although some of the best anywhere, had not really been made partners in the business. At the beginning of our first meeting, I set the stage and established an informal tone. Then, I began asking the employees true or false questions relating to competitiveness and productivity. That's it. It started out very simply.

As time passed, I developed the process more fully as a seven-step cycle. In this chapter you will learn how this process can be used to develop a big picture training program in your organization. But first, let's take a closer look at what Big Picture Training is and what it can do for your organization.

What Does Big Picture Training Accomplish?

What companies need today to be competitive is training that transforms the organization — that strategically and directly influences the direction, culture, and mindset of the organization. Big Picture Training can literally transform your entire organization. It can do informally what many formal programs cannot, because it consists of both organization development and training. Big Picture Training can accomplish many things at once:

- Help all employees feel a sense of active participation in the business.

- Help employees understand and assimilate organizational change in response to the outside world.

- Share the updated leadership vision for the organization.

- Share the central mission of the organization.

- Instill and reinforce core values and changing company culture.

- Provide insights and give more accurate perspectives on the business.

- Actively involve all employees in the thought process of the organization.

- Create productive information flow throughout the organization.

- Foster integration and continuous innovation.

- Teach fundamentals of change, customer focus, group problem solving, productivity, and quality improvement.

- Show needed connection across the organization.

- Help all employees understand the business possiblities.

- Encourage employees to share insights about how to improve the business

Getting Started

Big Picture Training requires that you identify key business and organizational issues in a way that is open and induces free-flowing conversation. I have used many different ways to generate focused discussion on issues important to the organization, including true/false quizzes, team focus worksheets, and something I call the Bug List (a form used to list the things that really bug you about the organization). Informality will set the stage for flexible thinking about change. Here are some of the issues that might be addressed early in the process to develop awareness and stimulate open discussion about the condition of the business.

- What does the "Big Picture" currently look like?

- What are the company's objectives?

- Which markets are expected to provide growth?

- Who is the competition? What are they doing? Why?

- Is your organization telling you what you need to know to be effective?

- Do corporate words and actions match? How great is the discrepancy? Why does it exist?

- What is the company's culture? Is it appropriate to the markets you service?

- Are you comfortable with the organization's public image?

- Do the company's values fit with your own?

- What types of behaviors seem to be rewarded by the organization?

- Do you respect the leaders of your organization? Why? Why not?

- Is the organization responsive to change?

- At what stage of maturity is the business?

- Is the company backward or forward-looking?

- What are the company's critical success factors?

- Where do you fit in tomorrow's organization?

- How can you best affect the "big picture"?

To initiate conversation in an early group session, I often share Peter Drucker's statement: "Unless challenged, every organization tends to become slack, easy-going, diffuse." This stimulates and encourages the sorting out of issues and motivations. It is also a first step toward building commitment. I will usually interject some kind of fun quiz that informs and becomes a basis for broadening perspectives.

Exploring the basics of productivity and a free market economy are generally useful in this informal process. A study of healthy and unhealthy organizations is an essential part as well. It is important that all organizational issues receive open, honest discussion in these small group sessions. The "company line" or corporate rhetoric is to be avoided. All issues are fair game for discussion when you are dedicated to becoming world-class. If the necessary openness and trust cannot be achieved, no change process will work.

Signs of Poor Organizational Health

- Consistent customer dissatisfaction

- Aging products/services

- Diminishing market share

- High turnover of employees

- Inflexible management

- Lack of communication flow between management and employee

- Inward-looking management

- Quality/reliability problems

- Top-heavy management

- Management out of rhythm with competition realities

- Poor employee relations

- Old-fashioned operating methods

Signs of Good Organizational Health

- Awareness and understanding of competition

- High responsiveness to customer needs

- Dedication to the quality the customer wants

- Regular flow of new products/services

- Appropriate pricing

- Enthusiastic employees

- Accessible management

- Flexible management

- Supportive financial controls

- Decentralized decision-making

- Focus on critical success factors

Choose A Facilitator

It is important to note the critical role of the person serving as facilitator of Big Picture Training. That person must have high credibility with both participants and top management. The individual must have an objective, independent perspective good interpersonal skills, and integrity to shape this process. Not everyone can or should lead this kind of effort. Be selective.

Go With The Flow

Also understand that the process, though structured, is very fluid and unpredictable. It unfolds differently each time it is used. Emphasis, pace, group dynamics, and outcomes will always be different. One thing is certain: it will improve the competitive position of the organization by improving productivity, building trust, improving communication, and reinforcing the interdependence of everyone in the organization.

At the beginning of the process, keep group sessions small and informative. Do not expect people to open up and share exceptional ideas without some "warming up" and experience with the process. After all, most companies have traditionally so inhibited productive thinking that it can sometimes take months for people to become constructive participants in the process.

Eliminate The Brain Line

Another barrier that must be broken down is the so-called "brain line." This is an invisible but very real line that each company draws — consciously or unconsciously

— through its organization to separate the "brains" (the people whose ideas are considered in the decision-making process) from the "hands" (as in "hired hands" or "warm bodies"). Thinking occurs on both sides of the line, of course, but in the typical company only thinking above the line has any weight in corporate decisions.

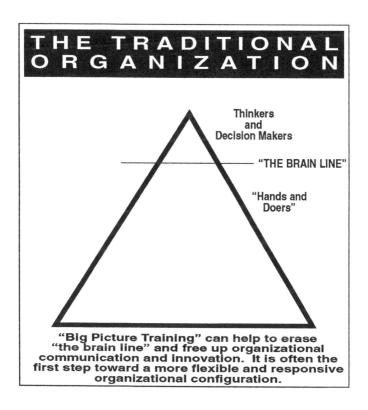

Recognizing that the line exists and initiating policies to eliminate it are important to Big Picture Training and absolutely essential if a company is serious about becoming and remaining a world-class competitor.

"Playing" With Change

Employees at all levels need a shared way of thinking about change. Because Big Picture Training is a fluid, flexible approach, it allows for a playful, creative, resourceful approach to effect changes. Most change or improvement efforts are not truly continuous in nature and are often too narrow in scope. Most formal or incremental programs will not work because they are formal and are thrust upon the organization rather than woven carefully from within. Also, most formal OD efforts don't really address the fluidity of change or subtle political realities in the organization. "Engineering" any major transformation requires a participative, *flexible* process, because change is not linear but rather organic and often unpredictable.

Effective training today is not just an integral part of organization development; it can and should be used to effect changes on patterns and results of the whole organization. Done properly, this kind of broad, orchestrated learning becomes a change strategy that can completely transform the organization. Rather than fighting over which OD "disciplines" will be used to engineer change, a common, flexible framework can be adopted. Executives, managers, and employees should not have to learn a whole new vocabulary to effect major change. Be pragmatic! Use whatever tools you need in a broad acceptable framework to get where you need to go. Don't worry about what to call it or whose model to follow. My experience has been that some of the most successful training programs are hybrid, adapted, or homespun anyway.

The Seven-Step Cycle

Experiment with Big Picture Training in your organization. Simply start where you stand to gain the most, and then use the seven-step cycle to help you get the most out of your Big Picture Training. The process is made up of the steps as shown in the illustration.

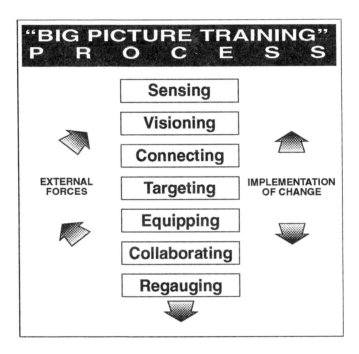

1. **Sensing**. In step one of Big Picture Training, all employees learn to "sense" what is happening in the world. Sensing consists of developing a much broader shared awareness and perspective. World-class employees are both outward-looking and forward-looking. The sensing step helps

discipline the whole organization to look beyond the walls of the workplace.

2. **Envisioning.** When leaders and followers are really in tune with the outside world, they can't help but get useful mental pictures of how things could be. That's what envisioning is all about. There is absolutely no way your management team is going to get where it wants to go without the clear articulation of a "future state" for the organization and without every employee understanding the vision.

3. **Connecting.** As soon as a cohesive, inspiring vision is shared with all employees, the "how to" question becomes the focal point. How do things happen? How should things happen? Who does what and why? Pivotal elements necessary for the vision are looked at closely during this phase of big picture training.

4. **Targeting.** Once people know how things fit together and who they are serving and why, then "targeting" becomes key. Targets — goals that will transform the vision into a reality — must be set by employees. How good people become at targeting will determine just how effective the company's total customer service is.

5. **Equipping.** Whether it is knowledge, information, or skills, people in the organization must be

provided the most useful tools possible to implement vision and strategies. Only after sensing, visioning, connecting, and targeting are completed, should equipping come into play, because it is a product of these other, fundamentally strategic, steps. However, equipping is obviously a critical step. Without it the previous phases may be worthless.

6. **Collaborating**. Processes for successful interdependence must be worked out. There is no magic model to work from, although some consultants might try to sell you on one model or another. Learning team process and team skills will do.

All employees need to learn these collaborative skills anyway. Even today, after so much emphasis on team building, many managers and executives have no idea how the team process really works. "Team" is more than just a nice popular buzzword for *people working well together.* For managers to forge effectiveness, they must do more than simply understand the term. You cannot appreciate the value of something if you don't fully understand it. You cannot capitalize on something you have not experienced or mastered. Inside today's most sophisticated and reputable corporations, managers still have much to learn. Attitudes that encourage comfort zones, the status quo, and "cover-your-rear" positions are all major obstacles to the open and fluid change process that must occur.

7. **Regauging**. In this step employees are continually altering behaviors, attitudes, and processes in order to respond to customer needs in a changing world. By involving all employees in this process, you help them to adapt effectively. You give them new agility through an innovative information flow and constant reality checks. You also send a clear message that continual internal change will be required to meet changing external challenges.

The Wave Of The Future

Mark Cummings, vice president of manufacturing for Case Datatel, calls Big Picture Training "the wave of the future." Problem solving and self-managing teams will become key to competitiveness. "Everything must go down to the lowest level," says Cummings. Changing mindsets, openness to new ideas, and flexibility are all critical aspects of training today." In 1990-91 Case Datatel focused on four broad goals: (1) quality improvement, (2) fast delivery, (3) innovation and fast cycle times, and (4) gross margin improvement. None of these goals can be achieved magically, mysteriously, or suddenly. To achieve them requires first, a process that is participative and customer-focused and second, investment in people through training — in other words, Big Picture Training.

With Big Picture Training, people begin to understand the central message of world-class training. The customer in the outside world is predominant. Seeing and understanding the big picture positions people for change and then equips them to deal with the changes most relevant to them. Big Picture Training reinforces the whole notion that training must be broad in scope and continuous in nature and, further, that training should be a strategic window on the world. Remember, a fully informed, well-connected, mission-driven workforce will win every time.

Chapter 7

A Practical Blueprint

7

A Practical Blueprint

"Ask the right questions and then get the organization to demand exceptional performance. Over the years, manufacturing reorganization and training programs have helped us the most."
— *George Fisher, CEO*
Motorola

Designing training courses has been the focus of many training professionals for years. Of greatest strategic importance, however, is the design of the total learning process. In this chapter you will learn about designing a blueprint for world-class training.

When I speak of a blueprint, I am not referring to instructional design or curriculum design. Instead, I'm talking about the overall game plan used in laying out world-class training, a process which is designed to help companies adjust to the rules, expectations, and competitive dynamics of this new world.

Elements Of A World-Class Blueprint

A world-class training blueprint must include the following elements to be effective:

- **An appreciation of the globalization process.** It is important to have a recognition of the events and forces that are reshaping the world and an understanding of the way business is conducted. World-class training is built on the premise that all training design starts in the global marketplace. As the world changes, skill and knowledge requirements change, often in revolutionary ways.

- **An integrated approach to organizational development.** The framework that I use for an integrated approach helps to show the interrelationship of business strategy, organizational planning, manpower planning, succession planning, career planning, training, education, and coaching.

- **A training design framework that is based on six strategic change levers.** I use this framework to design and implement the entire world-class training process, which is clearly a change process and not just an isolated training activity.

- **A training philosophy based on the company's strategic use of training to gain and keep competitive advantage.** This philosophy includes the following elements:
  - Learning is a never-ending process.
  - Effective training is a major source of competitive advantage.
  - Organization learning promotes organization-wide communication and reinforces corporate vision, values, and culture.
  - World-class training incorporates all this into a global context and integrates global knowledge and skills development.

- **A design process that is as much organization and strategy assessment as it is training needs assessment.** My approach to collecting information and assessing training and development needs is very direct and preferably informal. Only after getting to know several hundred people throughout the organization and sorting through information, perceptions, and opinions, can an implementer begin to effectively unfold a workable game plan. In design and implementation, it is essential to think and act using the same perception filters that your constituents or internal clients/business partner use—namely three—those of an executive business orientation, a middle manager, and a typical frontline employee. Of course, the reality is that to be effective you must relate to many different mindsets and personalities. I often use a modified critical events model developed by Len Nadler for basic needs assessment. Key questions in design surround the profiles of a world-class leader and a gold-collar workforce. Much of the content of any world-class training curriculum will be determined by organization members' "read" on how best to achieve this development given cultural and competitive realities.

- **Development and implementation that are integrated, rather than linear.** I use timelines, diagrams, targets, mission statements, and criteria, but in the end implementation is a very pragmatic, dynamic, and even crude process. What matters is whether or not it works and how powerful a change lever it becomes.

World-Class Design Options

The possibilities for world-class training designs are virtually endless depending on your business strategies. They could include courses, forums, round tables, briefings, seminars, and workshops on cultural issues, such as:

- Global account management

- Strategic alliance in the Pacific Rim

- World-class leadership

- Global project management

- Competition in the new Europe

- World-class negotiating

In connection with cultural training, you may need to have a fairly extensive foreign language series. This might include beginning, intermediate, and advanced courses in German, Spanish, Japanese, Russian, French, Italian, Czech, Hungarian, Serbo-Croatian, Swahili, Portugese, Chinese, and Korean. Use language training supplies that ensure effectively structured materials, excellent instructors, and a contextual or immersion approach to language learning. In implementing world-class training, always keep in mind the importance of remaining flexible, resourceful, and cost-effective. Never sacrifice quality, but try to ensure appropriate focus and depth in the learning design for each group you train. I tend to have between three to four alternative ways of conducting every course or seminar. Be open continually to suggestions about how to effectively conduct training programs throughout the organization.

To help you implement or evaluate your own world-class training process, I will provide a basic blueprint as a solid frame of reference. The three major components of the blueprint are: 1) the characteristics of a world-class training process, 2) the key elements or areas of coverage, and 3) specific examples of courses for each area.

First, the characteristics of such a process. How can you know whether you really have a world-class organizational learning process? There are six critical indicators. As shown on the graphic on the next page, the process must be globally oriented, well-marketed internally, results and behavior-oriented, comprehensive and integrated, innovative and flexible in implementation, and strategic in origin.

Finally, and above all, world-class training must provide a continuous stream of fresh global information, knowledge, and competencies through a "strategic window on the world." It is this global window of learning that drives the corporation forward and keeps it constantly adapting to its key customers and markets worldwide. Anything else is incremental, reactive, and virtually suicidal, competitively speaking.

Patterned after the Atomium in Brussels, this key graphic lays out the nine elements of world-class training. This molecular structure reflects the organic nature of learning in the global corporation showing the integration of disciplines and skills in a comprehensive framework that is flexible and nonhierarchal. (This same structure also provides an excellent example of multidimensional, global network organizations — the global corporation of the twenty-first century.) The nine critical areas of learning for the world-class corporation are: World-Class Leadership, Global Management Skills, Global Marketing, Global Sales and Service, Global Finance, Global Technologies, Global Telecommunications, Cross-Cultural Skills, and Foreign Language Skills. Without these competencies growing and adapting the company from the center out, there is no possibility of long-term competitiveness in most industries.

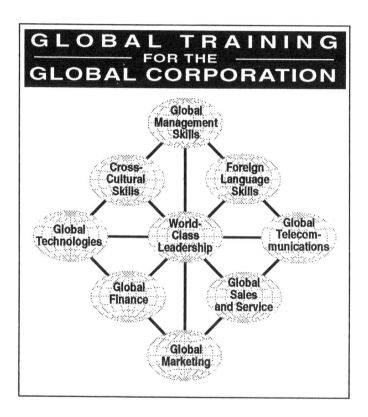

To more completely fill out the world-class training blueprint, here are some of the types of courses and programs which companies are using to reshape themselves and gain competitive advantage in the global marketplace.

WORLD-CLASS TRAINING™
GLOBAL [for] GLOBAL
LEARNING [the] CORPORATION

Cross-Cultural Skills

- Cross-Cultural Shortcourse
- Advanced Cross-Cultural Workshop
- Training Across Cultures
- Country-Specific Briefings

Global Management Skills

- The Global Manager
- Global Business Strategy
- Global Quality Management
- Project Management for the Global Corporation
- Managing the Multicultural Team

Foreign Language Skills

- English
- Japanese
- German
- Russian
- French
- Spanish
- Arabic
- Swahili
- Korean
- Thai
- Hindi
- Portuguese
- Hungarian
- Polish
- Greek
- Italian
- Chinese (Mandarin)
- Indonesian (Bahasa)

Global Technologies

- Simultaneous Engineering
- Just-In-Time Inventory
- Value-Added Manufacturing
- Flexible Manufacturing Systems
- Computer Integrated Manufacturing
- High-Velocity Production

World-Class Leadership

- The World-Class Leader
- The World-Class Supervisor
- Developing the World-Class Organization
- Global Perspectives on Leadership
- Ethics and the Global Executive
- Creativity and the Innovative Spirit

Global Telecommunications

- Briefing on Global Telecommunications
- Global Networks
- Distance Learning Systems
- Information Technology Update
- ISDN
- BISDN

Global Finance

- Global Trade and Finance Overview
- Import/Export
- Strategic Alliances

Global Marketing

- Managing the Global Marketing Organization
- Global Product Management
- Market/Industry Briefings
- Customer Profiling
- Competitor Profiling

Global Sales and Service

- Global Selling Skills
- International Negotiating
- Effective Sales Presentations Across Cultures
- World-Class Customer Service

To implement a process as powerful as world-class training that transforms an organization and its results so completely, a massive but subtle campaign is required. It is a fascinating blend of organizational re-engineering, organizational learning, and marketing. Those responsible for implementing the process must be ferocious learners; excellent marketers; and experts in organization development, business strategy, and human resource development. They must have a world-class leader profile themselves and know how to create the future of the enterprise. Generally, they are extremely intuitive, market- and idea-oriented, and highly people-skilled. They are constantly synthesizing and synergyzing information, ideas, systems, and people. These implementers must work closely with key leaders to ensure that politics and status quo don't get in the way of the corporate future and long-term competitive success.

As you go about this major undertaking, you will find yourself visioning, mapping, seeding, positioning ideas, packaging key events, intervening in organizational behavior patterns and values, networking (from top to bottom and sideways), identifying and cultivating sponsors and clients, and translating the shifting external reality into practical organizational learning.

The process of connecting and synthesizing all the information strands and political and personal realities that are a part of this process can be overwhelming at times, but the results of building an effective world-class training process are absolutely beyond imagination. Changes people and groups have needed to make for years finally find enough impetus and a change vehicle. Business opportunities in key and emerging markets come into view and focus, and new revenue flow is generated. New perspectives develop; broader mindsets prevail. Transactions across corporate lines improve. Global throughput and market responsiveness improve in leaps. People in the organization lock into a market reality and business mission they have internalized. World-class training becomes the high-octane fuel for which corporate leaders have been searching. World-class training is the global learning curve accelerator, individually and collectively. If your organization has not launched such a comprehensive globalized learning process, don't delay another week! The window of opportunity for staying in the global game may be closing as you read this. If you have been struggling to implement something similar, I want to encourage you with all my might to keep moving forward along the lines I have described. Do not give up! Keep going! Your efforts are more critical than you can possibly know.

I conclude with some snapshots of what several world-class companies are doing along the lines of world-class training.

COMSAT — A Blueprint

In 1990 COMSAT was awarded ASTD's prestigious International Training Award. When I began designing a world-class training initiative at COMSAT, the company had not conducted training for over two years. There was a hunger in the organization for developmental activity. As a result, it would have been easy to take a less strategic approach than I did and install piecemeal training that would simply pacify.

The approach we took was much more comprehensive and strategic than anyone imagined possible. In fact, there had been a number of less than successful training efforts prior to this one, and many thought that any approach would be short-lived. This was an excellent challenge. The first tasks would involve identifying critical strategic challenges and opportunities for the divisions and developing relationships at all levels of the organization.

To do basic needs analysis, I started gathering information from the chairman and his reports and then moved quickly to collect random input from front-line employees and middle managers. During about a four-month period, I collected information, ideas, and opinions from nearly 300 employees. This was an excellent base from which to begin synthesizing and designing. The content produced in this gathering phase was blended together carefully to meet many needs — developmental, motivational, and political. The content not only reflected what individuals thought but also what the competition was doing and what the customer wanted.

Initially, the content of the curriculum was not so globalized. Only after some leading questions, suggestions, and nudging did the scope of the training process become fully globalized. When I added training in cross-cultural skills, more language skills, and export/import and international negotiating, the curriculum began to directly address the impact of globalization. The emphasis on customer focus, total quality, innovation, global leadership, managing change, and cutting-edge technical and PC training, rounded out the process as one which was truly world-class. As business becomes global, corporations must make sure they are producing the most effective global employees possible. A world-class training curriculum helps to ensure this like nothing else can. No other process can develop an entire organization that thinks globally.

The mission of corporate training at COMSAT is to be a strategic resource to support the development and performance of all lines of business. This mission is reflected in its curriculum design, in operating responsiveness, and in related special projects.

COMSAT's final curriculum consisted of 75 courses in seven series:

- International

- Foreign languages

- Special programs

- Management

- Sales and marketing

- Technical/PC/telecommunications

- Administrative

Some of the individual course offerings include: global marketing, global telecommunications, world-class customer service, global leadership, world region updates, cross-cultural short course, international finance, German, Spanish, Japanese, and Russian.

As I was designing the curriculum, I was simultaneously identifying training resources, both internally and externally. About thirty volunteer instructors were identified among the top executives and technical experts of the company. I personally am able to conduct about 30 of the 75 courses, as appropriate, and the remainder are conducted by excellent external consultants and trainers. Only world-class suppliers stay on our roster of vendors.

While COMSAT's globalized training effort is nearly two years ahead of the closest competition, not every executive and employee understood the significance of globalized training at the exact same time. All major change is a gradual and "organic" process. We are always "in process." Everyone is at a different place of understanding and has a different perception of what is or isn't happening, depending on the level of involvement in the process.

COMSAT employees, both internally and externally, can tell you the company is more competitive and more energized. There is excitement about future business ventures around the globe. The organization is becoming more customer- and change-driven, and global skills are being instilled throughout the system. The benefits of world-class training are being realized now and will yield even greater rewards in the coming years as markets change and as employees are cultivated, challenged, and fully globalized.

AT&T
In 1988-89 global management curriculums were not easy to come by, but Nancy Burgas, then Manager of Global Training for AT&T in Basking Ridge, New

Jersey, had created a compact, but well-designed global development process. The learning process consisted of three levels: introductory, intermediate, and advanced. The introductory segment included Elements of Global Business, Managing a Global Business: Money and Results, and Cross-Cultural Business Negotiations and Communications. The intermediate level contained Strategies for Competing Globally, Tactics for Competing Globally, Finance in the Global Marketplace, and Product Management in Global Markets. The advanced session featured an advanced business simulation, Global Management.

This curriculum was the catalyst for many other global training initiatives across the company and has been fully integrated into the chairman's program, so that AT&T's top executives can stay high on the learning curve as globalization totally reshapes the dynamics of competition in their industry.

Honeywell

One of the first U.S. multinationals to reconfigure into a global corporation, Honeywell has addressed a number of people development and deployment issues in recent years. Michael Bonsignore, the ultimate global executive, has helped to lead Honeywell through this reshaping process. The result: strong worldwide business teams, better corporate performance, and an incredible array of customer partnerships across 90 countries throughout the globe.

Royal Bank Of Canada

Few banks outside of Japan have taken a more enlightened approach to global human resource development than

"The Royal." The amount of money invested annually in Royal Bank personnel through training and education is phenomenal, and the professionalism with which the HRD process is approached is virtually unmatched. One look at the company's training catalog makes this abundantly clear. Jim Gannon, senior vice president of Human Resource Planning and Development, is helping to support global business strategies with the appropriate level and type of personnel and executive opportunities. Every economic sector the bank serves is addressed by a well-conceived development program or seminar series (in French and English), and virtually every level or job category is included in the corporate-wide learning process.

Millipore

A relatively small company, Millipore still easily qualifies as global. Over 20 nationalities are represented in their broadly dispersed but tight-knit management team. They meet regularly and discuss business issues and vantage points across regions. Their training department, while not large, is very active and well-focused on making Millipore employees and managers effective worldwide. Jackie Jones, director of training, works to see that everyone has the tools and skills necessary to transact business, to market, and to lead across cultures. This company's efforts should be inspiring to many.

British Telecom

In an effort to implement Ian Valiance's global vision for BT, BT Americas Region has begun globalized training focused on global account management and cross-cultural issues in global marketing. Positioning aggressively for global marketshare, BT has much to gain by investing in this kind of implementation training.

AMP

AMP is a world-class supplier of electronic components, connectors, and semi-conductors to IBM, GE, GM, Hewlett-Packard, Sun Microsystems, Siemens, Daimler-Benz, and GE. The company has built its global reputation on advanced technology, solid financial management, and premium quality. To support this market position and reputation, they have invested heavily in engineering education, continuous quality improvement, and, more recently, in worldwide succession planning and global leadership development (or "globe-able" leader development, as Dr. Leonard Hill, director of human resource planning and executive development for AMP likes to refer to it). Few companies have taken as enlightened an approach to globalization. AMP is preparing its leaders and employees worldwide to operate more effectively across geographic and cultural boundaries.

Motorola

Motorola is another excellent example of a world-class company equipping for long-term global competitiveness. They have developed a reputation for world-class training, world-class quality (six sigma), and world-class manufacturing. If you look through Motorola's current corporate training catalog, it is obvious that this corporation is equipping its people for high performance in a fiercely competitive, global industry. John Robinson of Motorola University, himself multilingual, highlights two factors: 1) the language courses offered at the University Galvin Center, in cooperation with local universities, and 2) the number of non-Americans represented on the advisory boards for training and education across Europe, the U.S., and the Pacific Rim. Most impressive is the return on this massive investment in training and education. Motorola has positioned extremely well throughout the triad. They are already reaping the benefits of Bob Galvin's version of a "gold collar workforce."

NEC

For nearly 25 years, Nippon Electric Company has been doing something similar to globalized training. They have invested millions of dollars in the development of "global employees and managers," offering language training, background in international finance and economics, international law and insurance, as well as regional history and culture courses. Their investment supported their long-term global vision. Now you see the culmination of this farsighted investment in people — NEC's Global Strategy to dominate across two now-related industries — "Communications and Computers." The payoff continues to be high.

Each of these companies has recognized the necessity of thinking globally and investing in continual global learning. The success of your organization will depend on the extent to which you follow a similar course to ensure your organization is ready to meet the world-class challenge.

Bibliography

Chapter One — World-Class Training

Copeland, Lennie, and Lewis Griggs. *Going International.* Random House, 1985.

Harris, Philip, editor. *Global Strategies for Human Resource Development.* ASTD, 1984.

Kang, T.W. *Gaishi.* Basic Books, 1990.

Lessem, Ronnie. *Total Quality Learning.* Basil Blackwell, 1991.

Nadler, Leonard. *Designing Training Programs: The Critical Events Model.* Addison-Wesley, 1982.

Porter, Michael. *Competitive Advantage of Nations.* Free Press, 1990.

Chapter Two — World-Class Challenge

Barlett, Christopher, and Sumantra Ghoshal. *Managing Across Borders: The Transnational Solution.* Harvard, 1989.

Burnstein, Daniel. *Euroquake.* Simon & Schuster, 1991.

Crandall, Robert, and Kenneth Flamm, editors. *Changing the Rules.* Brookings, 1989.

Davidson, William, and Stanley Davis. *2020 Vision.* Simon & Schuster, 1991.

Davis, Stanley. *Future Perfect.* Addison-Wesley, 1987.

de Sola Pool, Ithiel. *Technologies Without Boundaries.* Harvard, 1990.

Dertouzos, Michael, Richard Lester and Robert Solow. *Made in America.* MIT, 1989.

Dicken, Peter. *Global Shift.* Harper, 1986.

Drucker, Peter F. *The New Realities.* Harper, 1989.

Grayson, C. Jackson, Jr., and Carla O'Dell. *American Business: A Two Minute Warning.* Free Press, 1988.

Groen, Janny, Efke Smit and Juurd Eijsvoogel, editors. *The Discipline of Curiosity: Science in the World.* Elsevier, 1990.

Halberstam, David. *The Next Century.* Morrow, 1992.

Ishihara, Shintaro. *The Japan That Can Say No.* Simon & Schuster, 1991.

Kennedy, Gavin. *Doing Business Abroad.* Simon & Schuster, 1985.

King, Alexander, and Bertrand Schneider. *The First Global Revolution.* Pantheon, 1991.

Kotkin, Joel, and Yoriko Yishimoto. *The Third Century.* 1988.

Lu, David. *Inside Corporate Japan.* Productivity, 1987.

Morita, Akio. *Made in Japan.* Penguin, 1988.

Naisbitt, John, and Patricia Aburdene. *Megatrends 2000.* Morrow, 1990.

Ohmae, Kenichi. *The Borderless World.* Harper, 1990.

Ozawa, Terutomo. *Multinationalism, Japanese Style.* Princeton, 1979.

Peters, Tom. *Thriving On Chaos.* Knopf, 1991.

Porter, Michael, editor. *Competition in Global Industries.* Harvard, 1989.

Reich, Robert. *The Work of Nations.* Knopf, 1991.

Toffler, Alvin. *Powershift.* Bantam, 1990.

Williams, Teagan, and Beneyto. *The World's Largest Market.* AMACOM, 1990.

Womack, James, Daniel Jones and Daniel Roos. *The Machine That Changed The World.* MIT; Harper, 1990.

Chapter Three — World-Class Leadership

Barker, Joel. *Future Edge.* Morrow, 1992.

Casse, Pierre. *Training for the Multicultural Manager.* SIETAR, 1982.

Chesanow, Neil. *The World Class Executive.* Rawson, 1985.

Cleary, Thomas. *The Japanese Art of War.* Random House, 1991.

Foster, Richard. *Innovation: The Attacker's Advantage.* Summit, 1986.

Green, Kenneth, and Daniel Seymour. *Who's Going to Run General Motors?* Peterson, 1991.

Harris, Philip, and Robert Moran. *Managing Cultural Differences: High Performance Strategies for Today's Global Manager.* Gulf, 1987.

Kouzes, James, and Barry Posner. *Leadership Challenge.* Jossey-Bass, 1987.

LeBoeuf, Michael. *GMP: The Greatest Management Principle in the World.* Berkley, 1985.

McCall, Morgan, Jr., Michael Lombardo and Ann Morrison. *The Lessons of Experience.* Lexington, 1988.

Miller, Lawrence. *Barbarians to Bureaucrats.* Potter, 1989.

Moran, Robert, editor. *Global Business Management in the 1990's.* Beecham, 1991.

Ozaki, Robert. *Human Capitalism: The Japanese Enterprise System as World Model.* Kondansha, 1991.

Rowan, Roy. *The Intuitive Manager.* Berkley, 1986.

Schlosstein, Steven. *The End of the American Century.* Cogdon & Weed, 1989.

Shook, Robert. *Honda: An American Success Story.* Prentice Hall, 1988.

Tichy, Noel. *Managing Strategic Change.* Wiley, 1983.

Tichy, Noel, and Mary Anne Devanna. *The Transformational Leader.* Wiley, 1990.

Chapter Four — Gold Collar Workforce

Clifford, Donald, Jr., and Richard Cavanagh. *The Winning Performance.* Bantam, 1985.

Hickman, Craig and Michael Silva. *Creating Excellence.* New American, 1984.

Holden, Jim. *Power Base Selling.* Wiley, 1990.

Kelly, Robert. *Gold Collar Employees.* AMACOM, 1985.

Leider, Richard. *The Power of Purpose.* Fawcett, 1985.

Ludeman, Kate. *The Worth Ethic.* Dutton, 1989.

Miller, Lawrence. *American Spirit: Visions of a New Corporate Culture.* Morrow, 1984.

Miller, William. *The Creative Edge.* Addison-Wesley, 1987.

Nelson, Rebecca, and David Clutterbuck. *Turnaround.* Mercury, 1988.

Noe, John. *Peak Performance Principles for High Achievers.* Berkley, 1984.

Sorenson, Head, Johnson, and Mathys. *International Organization Development.* Stipes, 1991.

Zemke, Ron, and Kristin Anderson. *Delivering Knock Your Socks Off Service.* AMACOM, 1991.

Chapter Five — Cross-Cultural Maze

Austin, Clyde. *Cross-Cultural Re-entry.* ACU Press, 1986.

Axtell. *The Do's and Taboos of International Trade.* Wiley, 1991.

Casse, Pierre. *Training for the Cross-Cultural Mind.* SIETAR 1981.

Christopher, Robert. *The Japanese Mind.* Ballantine, 1983

Clark, Rodney. *The Japanese Company.* Yale, 1979.

Engholm, Christopher. *When Business East Meets Business West: A Guide to Practice and Protocol in the Pacific Rim.* Wiley, 1991

Fisher, Glen. *Mindsets.* Intercultural Press.

Furnham, Adrian, and Stephen Boohner. *Culture Shock.* Routledge, 1989.

Haddad, Hassan, and Basheer Nijim, editors. *The Arab World: A Handbook.* Medina, 1978.

Hall, Edward T. *Beyond Culture.* Doubleday, 1981.

Hall, Edward T., and Mildred Reed Hall. *Hidden Differences: Doing Business With the Japanese.* Doubleday, 1987.

Hall, Edward T., and Mildred Reed Hall. *Understanding Cultural Differences.* Intercultural Press, 1990.

Harris, Philip, and Robert Moran. *Managing Cultural Differences.* Gulf, 1987.

Hendon, Donald, and Rebecca Angeles Hendon. *World Class Negotiating: Dealmaking in the Global Marketplace.* Wiley, 1990.

Holstein, William. *The Japanese Power Game.* Penguin, 1991.

Kato, Hiroki, and Joan Kato. *Understanding and Working with the Japanese Business World.* Prentice Hall, 1992.

Kohls, L. Robert. *Developing Intercultural Awareness.* SIETAR, 1981.

Kohls, L. Robert. *Survival Kit for Overseas Living.* Intercultural Press, 1984.

Kramer, Jane. *Europeans.* Penguin, 1988.

Krause, Axel. *Inside the New Europe.* Harper, 1991.

Laufer, Peter. *Iron Curtain Rising.* Mercury, 1991.

Mole, John. *When In Rome ... A Business Guide to Cultures & Customs in 12 European Nations.* AMACOM, 1991.

Morris, Charles. *The Coming Global Boom.* Bantam, 1990.

Riding, Alan. *Distant Neighbors: A Portrait of the Mexicans.*

Rowland, Diana. *Japanese Business Etiquette.* Warner, 1985.

Seelye, H. Ned. *Teaching Culture.* NTC, 1988.

Smith, Hedrick. *The New Russians.* Random House, 1991.

Storti, Craig. *The Art of Crossing Cultures.* Intercultural Press.

Tung, Rosalie. *The New Expatriates.* Ballinger, 1988.

Washington International Center/Meridian House International. *There is a Difference: 17 Intercultural Perspectives.*

Walmsley, Jane. *Brit-Think, Ameri-Think.* Penguin, 1987.

The WORLD Group. *Global Perspectives on Leadership.* 1992.

Chapter Six — Big Picture Training

Barker, Joel. *Future Edge.* Morrow, 1991.

Garfield, Charles. *Peak Performance.* Warner, 1984.

Miller, Lawrence. *American Spirit: Visions of a New Corporate Culture.* Morrow, 1984.

Myers, M. Scott. *Every Employee A Manager.* McGraw-Hill 1970.

Shapiro, Eileen. *When Corporate Truths Become Competitive Traps.* Wiley & Sons, 1991.

Thompson, Charles "Chic." *What a Great Deal.* Harper, 1992.

Chapter Seven — A Practical Blueprint

Bartlett, Christopher, and Sumantra Ghoshal. *Managing Across Borders: The Transnational Solution.* Harvard, 1989.

Holden, Jim. *Power Base Selling.* Wiley, 1990.

Kang, T. W. *Gaishi.* Basic Books, 1990.

McKenna, Regis. *Relationship Marketing.* Addison-Wesley, 1991.

Nadler, Leonard. *Designing Training Programs: The Critical Events Model.* Addison-Wesley, 1982.

Ward, Gary. *Rapid Development Training for Small Business.* Boswell, 1990.

Yip, George. *Total Global Strategy.* Prentice-Hall, 1992.